$$
\begin{array}{r}
2020 \\
- 1941 \\
\hline
79
\end{array}
$$

The TAO
of Emerson

THE TAO
OF EMERSON

THE WISDOM OF THE TAO TE CHING AS FOUND
IN THE WORDS OF RALPH WALDO EMERSON

*Edited and with an Introduction
by Richard Grossman*

Brush calligraphy by Chungliang Al Huang

THE MODERN LIBRARY

NEW YORK

For Red Schiller and for Shanti Norris

All philosophy, of East and West, has the same centripetence.

—Emerson, *Representative Men*

A NOTE TO THE READER

This is one book, but within it are two manuscripts. The first, printed in italics on the left-hand (verso) pages, is based on the classical 1891 rendition of the eighty-one verses of the sacred Chinese text known as the Tao Te Ching, credited to a sage called Lao Tse and translated by the British Sinologist James Legge. On the right-hand (recto) pages is the "second" manuscript (in roman type), the same eighty-one verses of the Tao Te Ching, interpreted in words culled and organized by me from the writings of Ralph Waldo Emerson, the great nineteenth-century American philosopher and poet.

The inspiration for creating these parallel texts comes from the epigraph to this book—"all philosophy, of East and West, has the same centripetence"—an observation recorded by Emerson in his essay on Plato when he was thirty-three years old, and already on the road to becoming "America's Founding Thinker." Centripetence, of course, refers to the tendency of energy to move or progress toward the center, to the essence of things. As Emerson later wrote, "the hero is he who is immovably centered," and as Lao Tse put it, "your inner being guard, and keep it free"—both men standing for what Emerson would later call the "infinitude of the human soul." This veneration of both the depths and heights of the human soul blossoms in their writings into a credo for the conduct of life that elevates quietude, self-awareness, humility, and reverence for the natural world to such a level that it has captivated and inspired generations of men and women. The values contained within the words these sages wrote, no matter how cryptic or mystical they may seem in some instances, have given rise to a kind of "spiritual anthropology," focused first on a site in ancient China housing a relic document over 2,500 years old, and second on a body of work created by a poet/philosopher in the quite early days of a new and animated country in the Western world. Each set of writings has captivated and inspired seekers to revisit them and probe their wisdom in search of a guiding personal truth.

This book is an effort to bring together these two kindred works. Using fragments of Emerson's writings ranging in length from a phrase to an entire passage, I have tried to construct new poetic interpretations of Lao Tse's words. It is not the intent of this rendition of the Tao Te Ching through the prose and poetry of Ralph Waldo Emerson to create an amusing word game by plundering the works of Emerson with a pair of scissors. Any great writer's words can, by such manipulation, be made to reproduce the work of any other writer.

In this instance, the process by which Emerson's writings are shown as parallel to the verses of the Tao Te Ching is one in which the shared sense and spirit and philosophy of the two men is displayed. To do this I spent a great deal of time immersed alternately in the work of the two authors, and recollecting the comparable thoughts I discovered in each. For instance, in Chapter 2 of the Tao Te Ching, which is intended to lay out the Taoist notions of complementarity (the yin/yang principle), a close student of Emerson thinks immediately of Emerson's essay "Compensation," devoted at least in part to the same idea: the universe is characterized by the sway between nonantagonistic, but opposite forces, "as: spirit, matter; man, woman; odd, even; motion, rest. . . ." Thus, Chapter 2 in my "translation" employs five sentences taken from the "Compensation" essay. But there is a deeper connection to be seen when the dedicated reader of Emerson recalls that he also explored this theme in other places: in his poem "Each and All," for instance, and in his address "The Method of Nature" as well as in his essay "Spiritual Laws." Thus, one or more sentences from those sources become the Emersonian "version" of the sacred Taoist text. Conversely, in my daily rereading of Emerson, I highlighted any phrase that for me had the ring of the Taoist master. In this latter process, for example, as I read the phrase, "I am a weed by the wall" in Emerson's essay "Circles," I heard immediately the reverberation of the self-deprecating tone of Lao Tse in Chapter 20, "I alone seem listless and still . . ."

The focus of this endeavor, then, is not so much on Lao Tse's and Emerson's similarities of verbal expression as it is on the wonderful ways in which philosophical ideas appear and reappear throughout history and across cultures, and are enriched in each new incarnation.

CONTENTS

LIST OF ILLUSTRATIONS

INTRODUCTION

Over 120 translations of the Tao Te Ching[1] have been published in English since 1891. It has lured a variety of Sinologists, poets, philosophers, scientists, and scholars to try again and again to plumb its cryptic, provocative text for deeper meanings and for nuances that might make the wisdom of Lao Tse either more accessible, more modern, or more personally relevant to the Western reader. Some have wished to make the poetry more pronounced; others have wanted to make the translation more precisely like the original Mandarin language; still others have tried to make the Tao Te Ching a more religious document, a kind of Taoist Bible.

Almost all the translators of the Tao Te Ching, including James Legge,[2] whose translation is used in this book, called their work "interpretations," acknowledging the enduring fact that it is impossible for the language of one tradition to provide exact verbal equivalents for all the creative ideas of another tradition. In *The Tao of Emerson* I have not had to be concerned with "verbal equivalency" because I have concentrated not so much on the words of the Tao Te Ching, but rather on the ideas embedded in them. I have taken this approach because, after many years of reading and studying both the ideas of Lao Tse, the rural mystic, and the works of the Sage of Concord, I have become convinced that in a mysterious but remarkable way, Ralph Waldo Emerson, a self-defrocked American minister of the nineteenth century, evolved a personal worldview and philosophical stance so parallel to the Tao Te Ching that his own oeuvre of over forty volumes of poetry, lectures, addresses, personal journals, and notebooks contains the essence of the sacred ancient text.

These two men, separated in history by almost 2,500 years, one a citizen of the world's oldest empire and the other of one of its youngest republics, were sages whose messages were remarkably alike: live the simple, tranquil life; trust your intuition; find and revere the spiritual grace in the natural world; act without self-assertion; commit no violence against living things or persons; try to harmonize with the ebb and flow of nature and circumstances—and above all, assure that there is a place in the world for humility, yielding, gentleness, and serenity.

One reason for their kinship may be found in the study of the prophetic tradition. The scholar Richard Groff, who describes prophets as "articulate mystics," had this to say:

> Through the ages resound the voices of the prophets, the authentic men. We may not know the tongue of the wise man, but we always recognize his voice. . . . Jesus, Buddha, Lao Tse, Socrates, Fox, Emerson—worked at the tasks they felt were laid upon them by a higher authority, tasks which they were not at liberty to set aside. For countless generations those seeking to find their way in darkness have found lamps in the lives of men like these. . . . Prophet, saint, sage, savior—the differences among them are lost amid their similarities. Forget the labels. Wisdom is where you find it.[3]

It seems to me that Emerson virtually reincarnated Lao Tse's wisdom in his own work, and that his brand of fresh, vigorous, homegrown English adds a radiant color to the words of Lao Tse. Emerson himself, in his essay "History," noted that "Nature is full of sublime family likenesses throughout her works . . . and there are compositions of the same strain to be found in the books of all ages." His own observation suggests that an Emersonian rendition of the Tao Te Ching might have a special resonance for the modern reader.

The Tao Te Ching—pronounced *dow* as in *dowel, der,* as in the slightly slurred last syllable of *under,* and *jing,* as in *jingo*—is a short and simple book filled with aphorisms, epigrams, folk wisdom, and what one writer has called "polemic proverbs," all concerned with the mystery and beauty of the universe, accompanied by profound advice on how human beings might negotiate that universe in a fruitful, peaceful, and ultimately transcendent way.

With the Holy Bible and the Bhagavad Gita, the Tao Te Ching is one of the three most translated books in all of human history, despite the fact that its authorship, its date, and the circumstances of its original publication are still debated among scholars worldwide. There is, however, no argument that it *was* published in ancient China, around 571 B.C., a fact confirmed as recently as 1993, when fourteen inscribed strips of bamboo containing about 40 percent of the known text (to which two translators, Roger T. Ames and David L. Hall, have given the title *The Great One Gives Birth to the Waters*) were discovered in a royal tutor's tomb at Guodian, near the city of Ying, once the capital of the southern kingdom of Chu.

What is also as certain as the physical history of the Tao Te Ching—a title that is generally taken to mean "The Classic Book of the Way and Its Power," or "The Classic Book of the Ultimate Reality and Its Ideal Manifestation"—is the universal magnetism it has exerted on readers for centuries. Whatever historical arguments surround its roots, the little more than five thousand words of its text have been consistently recognized as among the most provocative and inspiring mystic teachings ever written. Whether rendered as rhyming verses[4] or short chapters of prose, the cryptic, paradoxical, and yet simple and powerful text sets forth the central themes of Taoist thought as the British philosopher Bertrand Russell saw and admired them: "Production without possession, action without self-assertion, and development without domination." In our current age of spiritual questing, religious revisionism, and political and military conflicts, the Tao Te Ching continues to offer seekers a fascinating framework in which to pursue the paths to peaceful prosperity, the possibility of reincarnation, the confirmation (or disconfirmation) of the existence of the soul, the right way to govern with "a light hand," the "moral equivalent to war," and other eternal questions of life's meaning.

This great work continues to be a beacon for the modern reader even though the Tao Te Ching was written in an ancient Mandarin dialect that is no longer spoken, and the text arose in a cultural background even more different from our modern Western environment than contemporary China is. The thoughts of Lao Tse remain influential around the world, as witnessed, for example, by the continuing spread of interest in and practice of Zen Buddhism, which owes much of its groundwork to Taoist principles as offered in the Tao Te Ching. Likewise, millions of unaffiliated men and women who pursue a spiritual search for a deeper meaning to the human condition turn to the eighty-one verses or chapters that make up this classic.

The original text was divided into two parts, the first thirty-seven chapters being considered the "Upper" part, devoted to *Tao*, which is the supreme, cosmic, indestructible energy or universal force (or what, in theistic systems, is suggested by the word *God*). The second, or "Lower," part of forty-four verses deals with *Te*, the manifestation, the behavior, the shape and the power of the *Tao*. In purely

Western, modern terms we might say that *Tao* is what we call Nature, and *Te* is the way Nature works in her many forms and actualities. (*Ching* is the term designating a classic, or sacred text.)

The name Lao Tse (really "The Old Boy") was an honorific given a man who was probably born in a town some fifty miles south of the modern city of Shangchui; professionally he was an archivist, or Keeper of Royal Documents, in the dynasty capital of Loyang. His real name may have been Li Erh; posthumously he was given two additional honorific names: Tan (meaning "long-eared," and hence, wise) and the provocative appellation "Prince Positive." In spite of his modest, though respected, station in life, he was widely known as a sage, but despairing of the decadence of the dynasty, he chose to leave his homeland and head west. Legend has it that when he reached Hanku, the most formidable pass in all of China, his arrival had been foretold, and the Warden of the Pass, Yin-hsi, implored the great man for some instruction, whereupon Lao Tse gave him the Tao Te Ching, and continued on to unknown regions of the far west. This event is affectionately described by the playwright and poet Bertolt Brecht in his little-known work *Legend of the Origin of the Book Tao-Te-Ching on Lao-Tse's Road into Exile*, the last stanza of which is:

> But the honor should not be restricted
> To the sage whose name is clearly writ.
> For a wise man's wisdom needs to be extracted.
> So the custom man deserves his bit,
> It was he who called for it.[5]

But Emerson knew nothing of the charming legend of Lao Tse or the Taoist philosophy it spawned. The Tao Te Ching was not to be available in English until 1891, nine years after his death. Thus, if he ever even encountered the word *Tao* it was in his reading of Confucius, a man twenty years junior to Lao Tse, whose *Analects* is the literary and philosophical counterpoint to the Tao Te Ching, and whose followers dominated the social and political structure of China in the late sixth and early fifth century B.C. By that time, as Arthur Kirby has said, "Chinese wisdom expressed itself in the outward symbolical relation of each individual to the Emperor and the Tao, not in thoughts about the Tao; for the early spirit of Lao Tse had died in the letter. . . ."[6] The Confucianism Emerson read about and admired ("I am reading a better Pascal") was impressive to him because it appeared to emphasize civic duty, moral education, and "the efficacy of the good example of the superior man." And surely Emerson and Confucius were linked by their common belief in what Emerson once called "the infinitude of the Asiatic soul."

But in practice, Confucianism was not a philosophy to which Emerson could have wholly subscribed, since it was almost exclusively concerned with societal structure, worldly transactions, codified rules of behavior, and what might be called patriarchal politics. While many of these themes interested Emerson, they all fall into the realm of "Society," which for him was only a part of human reality, needing always to be counterpoised with "Solitude," wherein the richness of the spiritual life becomes possible. So it is with the contrast between Confucius and Lao Tse—the former standing for stern authority, official discipline, the pursuit of "fame and reputation," where the latter sees all these characteristics as "so many handcuffs and fetters," preferring to stress the connection between a transcendent Nature and the material diversity of the universe, or the well-known "ten thousand things."

The Chinese-American philosopher and scientist Lin Yutang saw this when he wrote in his authoritative *The Wisdom of China and India*, "Generally, the reader will find reading Chinese philosophers like reading the best intuitive passages in Emerson."[7] And Yutang was doubtless thinking primarily of Lao Tse, the author of the Tao Te Ching. For in all his work, Emerson the paradoxical ("the highest prudence is the lowest prudence"), Emerson the mystical ("the world is but the incarnation of a thought"), Emerson the existential ("You are you, and I am I"), Emerson the present-centered ("Life only avails, not the having lived"), Emerson the epigrammatist ("a foolish consistency is the hobgoblin of little minds") is not comparable to the ordered, compulsive positivist Confucius, but rather to the flowing, spontaneous lover of analogies and allusions, the naturalistic and mystic Lao Tse.

The Viennese cultural historian Egon Friedell caught these atavistic "Oriental" qualities of Emerson's personality and style in his book *A Cultural History of the Modern Age:*

> His spiritual rhythm reminds one . . . of the gentle flowing of a meadow stream that hollows its bed slowly and peacefully. . . . He holds his candle directly up to things and looks them straight in the face like a healthy man who is not cowed by learned traditions. . . . He is an absolute Impressionist in his style, his composition, and his thought. He never propounds his ideas in a definite, logical or artistic form, but always in the natural and often accidental order which they have in his head. . . .
>
> He knows only provisional opinions, momentary truths. . . . He begins to develop this or that view, and we think he is going on to weave it systematically, elucidate it from all sides, entrench it against all possible attack. But then, suddenly some alien picture or simile, epigram or *aperçu* strikes him full in the middle of his chain of thought, and the theme thenceforward revolves on quite a new axis. . . .[8]

This might be an exegesis of the Tao Te Ching itself, emphasizing as it does the loose presentation of sage ideas, the intuitive confidence, the informality and directness, the earthy frame of reference, and ultimately, the simplicity of the wise man. And again we are reminded of both Lao Tse and Emerson when Friedell says of the latter, "He stops still, listens to his heart, and writes as he listens. . . ."

Notes

1. Since 1976 the preferred method of romanizing the Chinese language has been the pinyin system, which renders Lao Tse as Laozi, and his book as the Dao De Jing (which is, in fact, the way the title is pronounced, even when written as the Tao Te Ching). Whenever Chinese words occur in this volume, I have chosen to use the older Wade-Giles system of Romanization because it was in use throughout the nineteenth century, when both James Legge and Emerson lived.

2. James Legge (1815–1897) was a near contemporary of Emerson, who was born in 1803 and died in 1882. The two never met on any of Emerson's visits to England. A Scotch-Presbyterian minister, Legge first went to China in 1839 as a missionary. For nearly thirty years he lived in various parts of China, where he studied and translated many of the great Chinese classics. This work culminated in his developing, with F. Max Muller, the monumental *Sacred Books of the East* series, published in fifty volumes between 1879 and 1891, of which Volume 39 is Legge's translation of the Tao Te Ching. Legge held the chair in Chinese language and literature at Oxford University for twenty years.

3. Groff, Richard. *Thoreau and the Prophetic Tradition.* Los Angeles: The Manas Publishing Co., 1961.

4. In this book both James Legge's translation of the Tao Te Ching and the version I have gleaned from the writings of Ralph Waldo Emerson are set mainly as free verse, following the custom in the vast majority of translations of Lao Tse's classic since the first one, written in Latin, in 1788.

5. Brecht, Bertolt. *Poems 1913–1956.* Edited by John Willett and Ralph Manheim with the cooperation of Erich Fried. London and New York: Methuen, 1980.

6. Christy, Arthur. *The Orient in American Transcendentalism.* New York: Octagon Books, 1978.

7. Lin Yutang. *The Wisdom of China and India.* New York: Random House, 1942.

8. Friedell, Egon. *A Cultural History of the Modern Age,* 3 vols. New York: Alfred A. Knopf, 1933.

THE TAO
OF EMERSON

玄之
又妙

The gateway
to
All Mystery

1.   *The Tao that can be trodden is not the*
        enduring and unchanging Tao.
The name that can be named is not the
        enduring and unchanging name.

Conceived as having no name,
        it is the Originator of heaven and earth;
Having a name, it is the Mother of all things.

Always without desire we must be found,
If its deep mystery we would sound;
But if desire within us be,
Its outer fringe is all that we shall see.

Under these two aspects
        it is really the same;
But as development takes place,
        it receives the different names.

Together we call them the Mystery.
Where the Mystery is the deepest
        is the gate of all that is subtle and wonderful.

1.   That great nature in which we rest,
           that Unity, that Over-Soul,
      Is an Immensity not possessed,
           and that cannot be possessed.

      The animal eye sees, with wonderful
           accuracy,
           sharp outlines and colored surfaces.
      To a more earnest vision,
           outlines and surfaces
           become transparent;
      Causes and spirits
           are seen through them.

      The wise silence,
           the universal beauty,
      To which every part and particle
           is equally related,
      Is the tide of being which floats us
           into the secret of nature;
      And we stand before
                the secret of the world.

2. *All in the world know the beauty of the beautiful,*
    And in doing this they have the idea of what ugliness is;
    They all know the skill of the skillful,
    And in doing this they have the idea of what
        the want of skill is.

    So it is that existence and non-existence give birth
        one to the other;
    Difficulty and ease produce each other;
    Length and shortness fashion out the figure of the other;
    Height and lowness arise from the contrast of
        the one with the other;
    Musical notes and tones become harmonious
        through the relation of one to the other;
    Being before and behind give the idea of
        one following another.

    Therefore the sage manages affairs without doing anything,
        and conveys his instructions without the use of speech.
    The work is done, but how no one can see;
    'Tis this that makes the power not cease to be.

2.   Each thing is a half, and suggests another thing
        to make it whole.
As: spirit, matter;
    man, woman; odd, even;
    in, out; upper, under;
    motion, rest; yea, nay.
All are needed by each one.
Nothing is fair or good alone;
To empty here, you must condense there.

A great man is always willing to be little;
The wise man throws himself on the side
    of his assailants;
Postpones always the present hour
    to the whole life,
Postpones talent to genius,
    and special results to character,
Is very willing to lose particular powers
    and talents
So that he gain in the elevation
    of his life.
Action and inaction are alike to the true.

3. Not to employ men of superior ability
        is the way to keep the people from rivalry among themselves;
    Not to prize articles which are difficult to procure
        is the way to keep them from becoming thieves;
    Not to show them what is likely to excite their desires
        is the way to keep their minds from disorder.

    Therefore the sage, in the exercise of his government,
        empties their minds, fills their bellies,
        weakens their wills and strengthens their bones.

    He constantly tries to keep them without knowledge
        and without desire,
    And where there are those who have knowledge,
        to keep them from presuming to act on it.
    When there is this abstinence from action
                good order is universal.

3. Nothing is secure but life, transition,
  the energizing spirit.
The one thing which we seek
  with insatiable desire
Is to forget ourselves, to be surprised
  out of our propriety,
To lose our sempiternal memory
And do something without knowing
   how or why.

No truth is so sublime but it may be
  trivial tomorrow.
People wish to be settled;
Only as far as they are unsettled
  is there any hope for them.

The poor and the low have their way
  of expressing the last facts of philosophy:
"Blessed be nothing. The worse things are
   the better they are."

4.   *The Tao is like the emptiness of a vessel;*
        And in our employment of it we must
            guard against all fullness.
        How deep and unfathomable it is,
            as if it were the Honored Ancestor of all things!

        We should blunt our sharp points,
        And unravel the complication of things;
        We should temper our brightness,
        And bring ourselves into agreement
            with the obscurity of others.
        How pure and still the Tao is, as if it would
            ever so continue.

4.   There is never a beginning,
      There is never an end
         to the inexplicable continuity of this web.
      System on system, shooting like rays,
         upward, downward,
            without center, without circumference.

      In the mass and in the particle,
      Nature hastens to render account of herself.
      Under every cause, another cause;
      Truth soars too high and dives too deep
         for the most resolute inquirer.

5.　　Heaven and earth do not act from any wish
　　　　to be benevolent.
　　They deal with all things as the dogs of grass
　　　　are dealt with.

　　May not the space between heaven and earth
　　　　be compared to a bellows?
　　'Tis emptied, yet it loses not its power;
　　'Tis moved again, and sends forth air the more.
　　Much speech to swift exhaustion lead we see;
　　Your inner being guard, and keep it free.

5.   We find nature to be the circumstance
        which dwarfs every other circumstance,
And judges like a god
      all men who come to her.

There is no end in nature,
But every end is a beginning;
There is always another dawn risen on mid-noon,
And under every deep a lower deep opens.

Good as is discourse,
Silence is better, and shames it.

6.   *The valley spirit dies not, aye the same;*
       The female mystery thus do we name,
       Its gate, from which at first they issued forth,
       Is called the root from which grew heaven and
           earth.
       Long and unbroken does its power remain,
       Used gently, and without the touch of pain.

6.   In showers, in sweeping showers, the Spring
             visits the valley,
         The miracle of generative force,
         Far-reaching concords of astronomy.

         Nature is transcendental,
             ever works and advances.
         It is undefinable, unmeasurable,
         But we know that it pervades and contains us.

7.   *Heaven is long enduring and earth continues long.*
The reason why heaven and earth are able to endure
    and continue thus long
Is because they do not live of, or for, themselves.
This is how they are able to continue and endure.

Therefore the sage puts his own person last,
And yet it is found in the foremost place;
He treats his person as if it were foreign to him,
And yet that person is preserved.
Is it not because he has no personal and private ends,
    that therefore such ends are realized?

7. The universe is represented in an atom
     in a moment of time.
   It calls the light its own, and feels
     that the grass grows and the stone falls,
   Yet takes no thought for the morrow.

   Genius and virtue predict in man
     the same absence of private ends,
     and of condescension to circumstance,
   United with every trait and talent
     of beauty and power.
   The path which the hero travels alone
     is the highway of health and benefit to mankind.
   What is the privilege and nobility of our nature
     but its persistency,
   Through its power to attach itself
     to what is permanent?

8. *The highest excellence is like that of water.*
The excellence of water appears in its benefiting all things,
   and in its occupying, without striving,
   the low place which all men dislike.
Hence its way is near to that of the Tao.

The excellence of a residence is in the suitability of the place;
   that of the mind is in abysmal stillness;
   that of associations is in their being with the virtuous;
   that of government is in its securing good order;
   that of the conduct of affairs is in its ability;
   and that of any movement is in its timeliness.

And when one with the highest excellence
Does not wrangle about his low position,
   no one finds fault with him.

8.   Justice is the rhyme of things;
Trade and counting use
The self-same tuneful muse.

Water was the beginning of all things.
It is in that same liquid state
   that substances unite to
   and identify themselves with organized bodies.

The aim of the wise man will always be
   to set his time on such a key as he can hold,
   to bring his life level with the laws of the mind,
       not the body.

9.   *It is better to leave a vessel unfilled*
        than to attempt to carry it when it is full.
    If you keep feeling a point that has been sharpened,
        the point cannot long preserve its sharpness.

    When gold and jade fill the hall,
        their possessor cannot keep them safe.
    When wealth and honors lead to arrogance,
        this brings its evil on itself.
    When the work is done, and one's name
        is becoming distinguished,
                to withdraw into obscurity
                is the way of Heaven.

9.   All the toys that infatuate men—
            houses, land, money, luxury,
            power, fame—
        are the self-same thing.

        The man whose eyes are nailed,
            not on the nature of his act,
        But on the wages, whether it be
            money or office or fame,
            is equally low.

        Nature arms each man with some faculty
            which enables him to do easily
            some feat impossible to any other,
        And this makes him necessary to society.

        The peril of every fine faculty
            is the delight of playing with it for pride.

10.   When the intelligent and animal souls are held together
          in one embrace,
      They can be kept from separating.
      When one gives undivided attention to the vital breath,
          and brings it to the utmost degree of pliancy,
      He can become as a tender babe.
      When he has cleansed away the most mysterious sights
          of his imagination,
      He can become without a flaw.

      In loving the people and ruling the state,
          cannot he proceed without any purposeful action?
      In the opening and shutting of his gates of heaven,
          cannot he do so as a female bird?
      While his intelligence reaches in every direction,
          Cannot he appear to be without knowledge?

      The Tao produces all things and nourishes them;
      It produces them and does not claim them as its own.
      It does all, and yet does not boast of it;
      It presides over all, and yet does not control them.
      This is what is called the Mysterious Quality of the Tao.

10.   By yielding to the spirit which is innate
        in every man,
Canst thou silent lie?
Canst thou, thy pride forgot, like nature
        pass into the winter night's
        extinguished mood?
Canst thou shine now, then darkle?
And being latent feel thyself no less?
Wilt thou not open thy heart to know
What rainbows teach and sunsets show?
But you must have the believing and prophetic eye.

Respect the child.
Be not too much his parent.
Trespass not on his solitude.
Have the self-command you wish to inspire.

11.   *The thirty spokes unite in the one nave;*
            but it is on the empty space
            that the use of the wheel depends.
     Clay is fashioned into vessels;
            but it is on their empty hollowness
            that their use depends.
     Doors and windows are cut out to form an apartment;
            but it is on the empty space within
            that its use depends.
     Therefore, what has a positive existence serves
            for profitable adaptation,
     And what has not that for actual usefulness.

11.   An inevitable dualism bisects nature;
        If the south attracts, the north repels.

        What we gain in power is lost in time.
        If the good is there, so is the evil.
        If the affinity, so the repulsion.
        If the force, so the limitation.
        All things are double, one against another.

        Whilst the world is thus dual,
            so is every one of its parts.
        The entire system of things
            gets represented in every particle.

12.   *Color's five hues from th' eyes their sight*
            will take;
        Music's five notes the ears as deaf can make;
        The flavors five deprive the mouth of taste;
        The chariot course, and the wild hunting waste
        Make mad the mind; and objects rare and strange,
        Sought for, men's conduct will to evil change.

        Therefore the sage seeks to satisfy the craving
            of the belly,
        And not the insatiable longing of the eyes.
        He puts from him the latter,
            and prefers to seek the former.

12.   As soon as leisure plays with resemblances
             for amusement,
      We call its action Fancy.
      Fancy relates to surfaces,
        is willful, superficial,
      A play as with dolls and puppets.
      Fancy surprises and amuses the idle,
         but is silent in the presence of great passion.

      We must learn the homely laws of fire and water.
      We must feed, wash, plant, build.
      These are the ends of necessity,
        and first in the order of nature,
        the house of health and life.

13.   *Favor and disgrace would seem equally to be feared;*
        Honor and great calamity,
            to be regarded as personal conditions of the same kind.

        What is meant by speaking thus of favor and disgrace?
        Disgrace is being in a low position after the enjoyment of favor.
        Getting that favor leads to the apprehension of losing it,
            and losing it leads to the fear of still greater calamity—
        This is what is meant by saying that favor and disgrace
            would seem equally to be feared.

        And what is meant by saying that honor and great calamity
            are to be regarded as personal conditions?
        What makes me liable to great calamity is my having the body,
            which I call myself;
        If I had not the body, what great calamity could come to me?

        Therefore, he who would administer the kingdom,
        Honoring it as he honors his own person,
            may be employed to govern it.
        And he who would administer it with the love
            which he bears to his own person may be entrusted with it.

13. Blame is safer than praise.
Every sweet hath its sour, every evil its good.

Do men desire the more substantial
    and permanent grandeur of genius?
Neither has this an immunity.
He who by force of will or of thought is great
    has the charges of that eminence.
With every influx of light comes new danger.
Has he light? He must bear witness
    to that light
And always outrun that sympathy
    which gives him such keen satisfaction.

Welcome evermore to gods and men
    is the self-helping man.
For him, all doors are flung wide:
Him all tongues greet, all honors crown,
    all eyes follow with desire.

14. *We look at it, and we do not see it, and we name it*
         the Equable.
     We listen to it, and we do not hear it, and we name it
         the Inaudible.
     We try to grasp it, and we do not get hold of it, and we name it
         the Subtle.
     With these three qualities, it cannot be made the subject
         of description;
     And hence, we blend them together and obtain The One.

     Its upper part is not bright, and its lower part is not obscure.
     Ceaseless in its action, it yet cannot be named, and then
         it again returns and becomes nothing.
     This is called the Form of the Formless,
         and the Semblance of the Invisible;
     This is called the Fleeting and Indeterminable.

14.   The true order of nature beholds the visible
          as proceeding from the invisible.
      The rushing stream will not stop
          to be observed;
      So old and so unutterable,
      It is inexact and boundless.
      But all the uses of nature admit of being
          summed in one.

      Here about us coils forever
          the ancient enigma.
      It is faithful to the cause
          whence it had its origin.
      It is a perpetual effect,
      A great shadow pointing always
          to the sun behind us.
      How silent, how spacious, what room for all,
          yet without place to insert an atom;
      It will not be dissected, nor unraveled,
          nor shown.
      We learn that behind nature,
          throughout nature,
      Spirit is present, one and not compound;
      The history of the genesis of the old mythology
          repeats itself.

15. The skillful masters in old times,
        with a subtle and exquisite penetration,
    Comprehended its mysteries and were deep
        so as to elude men's knowledge.
    As they were thus beyond men's knowledge,
    I will make an effort to describe what sort
        they appeared to be.

    Shrinking looked they, like those
        who wade through a stream in winter;
    Irresolute like those who are afraid of all around them;
    Grave like a guest in awe of his host;
    Evanescent like ice that is melting away;
    Unpretentious, like wood
        that has not been fashioned into anything
    Vacant like a valley and dull like muddy water.

    Who can make the muddy water clear?
    Let it be still, and it will gradually become clear.
    Who can secure the condition of rest?
    Let movement go on,
        and the condition of rest will gradually arise.
    They who preserve this method of the Tao
        do not wish to be full of themselves.
    It is through their not being full of themselves
        that they can afford to seem worn and not appear
                    new and complete.

15.   In all nations there are minds which incline
         to dwell in the conception of the fundamental Unity.
      The world is upheld by the veracity of great men;
      They make the earth wholesome.
      Those who live with them find life glad and nutritious.
      What they know, they know for us.
      With each new mind, a new secret of nature transpires.

      Great men are then a collyrium to clear our eyes
         from egotism,
      And enable us to see other people and their works.
      They teach us the qualities of primary nature—
         admit us to the constitution of things.
      The escape from all false ties.
      Courage to be what we are
      And love what is simple and beautiful.
               These are the essentials.

      But true genius seeks to defend us from itself.
      True genius will not impoverish,
         but will liberate and add new senses.
      He is great who is what he is from nature
         and who never reminds us of others.
      The hero is he who is immovably centered.

16.	*The state of vacancy should be brought to the utmost degree,*
	and that of stillness guarded with an unwearying vigor.
All things alike go through their processes of activity,
And then we see them return to their original state.
When things in the vegetable world
	have displayed their luxuriant growth,
We see each of them return to its root.
This returning to their root is what we call
	the state of stillness;
And that stillness may be called a reporting
	that they have fulfilled their appointed end.

The report of that fulfillment is the regular, unchanging rule.
To know that unchanging rule is to be intelligent;
Not to know it leads to wild movements and evil issues.
The knowledge of that unchanging rule produces
	a capacity and forbearance,
And that capacity and forbearance lead to a community
	of feeling with all things.
From this community of feeling comes a kingliness of character;
And he who is king-like goes on to be heaven-like.
In that likeness to heaven, he possesses the Tao.
Possessed of the Tao, he endures long; and to the end
	of his bodily life, is exempt from all danger of decay.

16.   Then retire and hide,
            and from the valley
        Behold the mountain.
        Have solitary prayer and praise.
        Real action is in silent moments,
            in a thought which revises
            our entire manner of life.

        Be the lowly ministers of the pure omniscience.
        The sanity of man needs the poise of
            this immanent force.
        His nobility needs the assurance of
            this inexhaustible power.
        If he listens with insatiable ears,
            richer and greater wisdom is taught him.
        He is borne away as with a flood.
        His health and greatness consist
            in his being the channel
            through which heaven flows to earth.

        He who knows this most, he who knows
            what sweets and virtues are in the ground,
        The waters, the plants, the heavens,
        And who knows how to come at these enchantments
            is the rich and royal man.

17.   *In the highest antiquity, the people*
          did not know that there were rulers.
       In the next age they loved them and praised them.
       In the next they feared them; in the next they despised them.
       Thus it was that when faith in the Tao was deficient in the rulers,
          a want of faith in them ensued in the people.

       How irresolute did those early rulers appear,
          showing by their reticence the importance
          which they set upon their words!
       Their work was done and their undertakings were successful,
          while the people said, "We are as we are, of ourselves!"

17.   The old statesman knows that society is fluid;
        There are no such roots and centers;
        But any particle may suddenly become
            the center of the movement.

        The wise know that foolish legislation
            is a rope of sand,
            which perishes in the twisting;
        That the state must follow, and not lead
            the character and progress of the citizen.

        The appearance of character makes the state unnecessary.
        The wise man is the state.

18.   *When the great Tao ceased to be observed,*
            benevolence and righteousness came into vogue.
        Then appeared wisdom and shrewdness,
            and there ensued great hypocrisy.

        When harmony no longer prevailed
            throughout the six kinships,
            filial sons found their manifestation;
        When the states and clans fell into disorder,
            loyal ministers appeared.

18.   Society gains nothing whilst a man,
          not himself renovated,
      Has become tediously good in one particular
          but negligent or narrow in the rest.

      Hypocrisy is the attendant of false religion.
      When people imagine that others
          can be their priest,
      Whenever they understand that no religion
          can do them any more good than
          they actually taste,
      They have done fearing hypocrisy.

19.   *If we could renounce our sageness*
          and discard our wisdom,
             it would be better for the people a hundredfold.
       If we could renounce our benevolence
          and discard our righteousness,
             the people would again become filial and kindly.
       If we could renounce artful contrivances
          and discard our schemes for gain,
             there would be no thieves or robbers.

       Those three methods of government
       Thought old of ways in elegance did fail
       And made these names their want of worth to veil;
       But simple views, and courses plain and true
       Would selfish ends and many lusts eschew.

19.   The inner life sits at home,
            and does not learn to do things.
        It loves truth because it is itself real,
            it knows nothing else;
        But it makes no progress, was as wise
            in our final memory of it as now.
        It lives in the great present;
        It makes the present great.
        This tranquil, well-founded, wide-seeing soul
            is no express-rider, no attorney, no magistrate.
        It lies in the sun and broods on the world.

20. When we renounce learning we have no troubles.
     The ready "yes" and the flattering "yea"—
     Small is the difference they display.
     But mark their issues good and ill—
     What space the gulf between shall fill?

     The multitude of men look satisfied and pleased;
     As if enjoying a full banquet, as if mounted on a tower
          in spring.
     I alone seem listless and still, my desires having as yet
          given no indication of their presence.
     I am like an infant which has not yet smiled.
     I look dejected and forlorn,
          as if I had no home to go to.
     The multitude of men all have enough and to spare.
     My mind is that of a stupid man; I am in a state of chaos.

     Ordinary men look bright and intelligent, while I alone
          seem benighted.
     They look full of discrimination, while I alone
          am dull and confused.
     I seem to be carried about as on the sea, drifting as if
          I had nowhere to rest.
     All men have their spheres of action, while I alone
          seem dull and incapable, like a rude borderer.

     Thus I alone am different from other men, but I
               value the Tao.

20.   Away profane philosopher!
       Seekest thou in nature the cause?
       This refers to that, and that to the next,
       And the next to the third, and everything refers.

       The world rolls, the din of life
           is never hushed,
       The carnival, the masquerade is at its height;
       Nobody drops his domino.

       But I am only an experimenter;
       Do not set the least value on what I do
           or the least discredit on what I do not,
       As if I pretended to settle anything as true or false;
       I unsettle all things.

       No facts are to me sacred, none are profane.
       I simply experiment, an endless seeker,
           with no past to my back.
       I am a weed by the wall.
       I see that I am a pensioner, not a cause,
           but a surprised spectator of this ethereal water;
       That I desire and look up,
       And put myself in the attitude of reception;
       But from some alien energy,
           the visions come.

21.   The grandest forms of active force
       From the Tao come, their only source.
       Who can of Tao the nature tell?
       Our sight it flies, our touch as well.
       Eluding sight, eluding touch,
       The forms of things all in it crouch;
       Eluding touch, eluding sight,
       There are their semblances, all right.
       Profound it is, dark and obscure;
       Things' essences all there endure.
       Those essences the truth enfold.
       Of what, when seen, shall then be told.
       Now it is so; 'twas so of old.
       Its name—what passes not away;
       So, in their beautiful array,
       Things form and never know decay.

21.   There are no fixtures in nature;
The universe is fluid and volatile.
There is no outside, no inclosing wall,
    no circumference to us.
Every natural fact
    is a symbol of some spiritual fact.
The sage, until he hit the secret,
Would hang his head for shame,
But our brothers have not read it;
No one has found the key.

Thus there is no sleep, no pause,
    no preservation,
But all things renew, germinate
    and spring.

22.　*The partial becomes complete; the crooked, straight;*
　The empty, full; the worn-out, new.
　He whose desires are few gets them;
　He whose desires are many goes astray.

Therefore the sage holds in his embrace
　the one thing, humility, and manifests it to all the world.
He is free from self-display, and therefore he shines;
From self-assertion, and therefore he is distinguished;
From self-boasting, and therefore his merit is acknowledged;
From self-complacency, and therefore he acquires superiority.
It is because he is thus free from striving
　that therefore no one in the world is able to strive with him.

That saying of the ancients
　that "the partial becomes complete" was not vainly spoken—
All real completion is comprehended under it.

22.   Those who are capable of humility,
            of justice, of love, of aspiration,
        Stand already on a platform that commands
            action and grace.
        This energy did not descend into individual life
            on any other condition
            than entire possession.

        It comes to the lowly and the simple;
        It comes to whomsoever will put off
            what is foreign and proud;
        It comes as insight, it comes as
            serenity and grandeur.

23.   *Abstaining from speech marks him who is obeying*
            the spontaneity of his nature.
       A violent wind does not last for a whole morning;
       A sudden rain does not last for the whole day.
       To whom is it that these two things are owing?
       To heaven and earth.
       If heaven and earth cannot make such actions last long,
            how much less can man!

       Therefore, when one is making the Tao his business,
       Those who are also pursuing it, agree with him in it,
       And those who are making the manifestation of its course
            their object agree with him in that;
       While even those who are failing in both these things
            agree with them where they fail.

       Hence, those with whom he agrees as to the Tao
            have the happiness of attaining to it;
       Those with whom he agrees as to its manifestation
            have the happiness of attaining to it;
       And those with whom he agrees in their failure
            have also the happiness of attaining to the Tao.
       But when there is not faith sufficient on his part,
       A want of faith in him ensues on the part of the others.

23.   Silence is better than speech.

All things are in contact,
Every atom has a sphere of repulsion.
For nature, who abhors maneuvers,
    has set her heart on breaking up all styles and tricks.
Nature keeps herself whole,
    and her representation complete.

In splendid variety these changes come,
    all putting questions to the human spirit.
Those men who cannot answer by a superior wisdom
    these facts or questions of time, serve them.
Facts encumber them, tyrannize over them,
    and make the men of routine the men of sense,
In whom a literal obedience to fact
    has extinguished every spark of that light
    by which man is truly man.

But if the man is true to his better instincts
    or sentiments, and refuses the dominion of facts,
As one that comes of a higher race
    remains fast by the soul and sees the principle,
Then the facts fall aptly and supple
    into their places;
They know their master, and the meanest of them
    glorifies him.

24.   *He who stands on his tiptoes does not stand firm;*
         He who stretches his legs does not walk easily.
         So, he who displays himself does not shine;
         He who asserts his own views is not distinguished;
         He who vaunts himself does not find his merit acknowledged;
         He who is self-conceited has no superiority allowed to him.
         Such conditions, viewed from the standpoint of the Tao,
         Are like remnants of food, or tumors on the body,
             which all dislike.
         Hence those who pursue the Tao do not adopt and allow them.

24. If a man lose his balance, and immerse
           himself in any trades and pleasures
           for their own sake,
    He may be a good wheel or pin,
    But he is not a cultivated man.
    The man of the world avoids all brag.

    Prudence consists in avoiding and going without,
           not in the inventing of means and methods,
           not in adroit steering, not in general repairing.
    Such is the value of these matters
    That a man who knows other things,
           can never know too much of these.

25.   There was something undefined and complete,
         coming into existence before Heaven and Earth.
      How still it was and formless,
         standing alone, and undergoing no change,
         reaching everywhere and in no danger of being exhausted!
      It may be regarded as the Mother of all things.

      I do not know its name, and I give it the designation of the Tao
         (the Way or Course).
      Making an effort to give it a name
         I call it the Great.

      Great, it passes on in constant flow.
      Passing on, it becomes remote.
      Having become remote, it returns.
      Therefore, the Tao is great;
      Heaven is great; Earth is great;
      And the sage is also great.
      In the universe there are four that are great,
      And the sage is one of them.

      Man takes his law from the Earth;
      The Earth takes its law from Heaven;
      Heaven takes its law from the Tao.

      The law of the Tao is its being what it is.

25. For the world was built in order
And the atoms march in tune,
Rhyme the pipe, and time the warder,
The sun obeys them and the moon.

We cannot learn the cipher
That's writ upon our cell.
Stars taunt us by a mystery
Which we could never spell.

The conscious stars accord above,
the waters wild below.
For nature listens in the rose
and hearkens in the berry's bell.
There is a melody born of melody
which melts the world into a sea.
Nature is a mutable cloud,
Which is always and never the same.

Nothing divine dies.
The beauty of nature reforms itself in the mind,
and not for barren contemplation, but for new creation.

26.   *Gravity is the root of lightness;*
        stillness, the ruler of movement.

        Therefore, a wise prince, marching the whole day,
            does not go far from his baggage wagons.
        Although he may have brilliant prospects to look at,
            he quietly remains in his proper place,
            indifferent to them.
        How should the lord of a myriad chariots
            carry himself lightly before the kingdom?
        If he do act lightly, he has lost his root;
        If he proceed to active movement,
            he will lose his throne.

26. The fact of two forces, centripetal and centrifugal,
      is universal.
   And each force by its own activity
      develops the other.
   Nature will not have us fret and fume.
   Our painful labors are unnecessary and fruitless.
   Only in our easy, simple, spontaneous action
      are we strong.
   There is no need of struggle, convulsions,
      and despairs,
   Or the wringing of hands and the gnashing of teeth.
   We miscreate our own evils.

27.   The skillful traveler leaves no traces
            of his wheels or footsteps;
    The skillful speaker says nothing
            that can be found fault with or blamed;
    The skillful reckoner uses no tallies;
    The skillful closer needs no bolts or bars,
            while to open what he has shut will be impossible;
    The skillful binder uses no strings or knots,
            while to unloose what he has bound will be impossible.

    In the same way the sage
            is always skillful at saving men,
    And so he does not cast away any man;
    He is always skillful at saving things,
    And so he does not cast away anything.
    This is called "hiding the light of his procedure."

    Therefore, the man of skill is a master to be looked up to
            by him who has not the skill;
    And he who has not the skill is the helper
            of the reputation of him who has the skill.
    If the one did not honor his master,
            and the other did not rejoice in his helper,
    An observer, though intelligent, might greatly err about them.
    This is called "the utmost degree of mystery."

27.   'Tis as easy to twist iron anchors,
        and braid cannons, as to braid straw,
    To boil granite, as to boil water,
        if you take all steps in order.

    By simple living, by an illimitable soul,
        you inspire, you correct, you instruct,
        you raise, you embellish all.
    By your own act, you teach the beholder
        how to do the practicable.
    According to the depth from which you
        draw your life,
    Such is the depth of your manners and presence.

    By the permanence of nature,
        minds are trained alike,
    And are made intelligible to each other.

    Good is a good doctor, but Bad is sometimes a better.

28.   *Who knows his manhood's strength,*
        Yet still his female feebleness maintains;
        As to one channel flow the many drains,
        All come to him, yea, all beneath the sky.
        Thus he the constant excellence retains—
        The simple child again, free from all stains.

        Who knows how white attracts:
        Yet always keeps himself within black's shade,
        The pattern of humility displayed,
        Displayed in view of all beneath the sky;
        He in the unchanging excellence arrayed,
        Endless return to man's first state has made.

        Who knows how glory shines,
        Yet loves disgrace, nor e'er for it is pale;
        Behold his presence in a spacious vale,
        To which men come from all beneath the sky,
        The unchanging excellence completes its tale;
        The simple infant man in him we hail.

28.   Men of genius are said to partake of
            the masculine and feminine traits.
        As much as a man is a whole,
            so is he also a part.
        Speak as you think, be what you are,
        Look upon the simple and childish virtues
            of veracity and honesty
            as the root of all that is sublime in character.
        A multitude of trifles impede the mind's eye
            from the great search
            of that fine horizon-line that truth keeps.
        The way to knowledge and power
            is not through plenty and superfluity,
        But by denial and renunciation
            into solitude and privation.
        Let us apply to this subject the same torch
            by which we have looked at all
            the phenomena of the time,
        The infinitude, namely, of every man.
        Everything teaches that.

29.   *If anyone should wish to get the kingdom for himself,*
            and to effect this by what he does,
        I see that he will not succeed.
        The kingdom is a spirit-like thing,
            and cannot be got by active doing.
        He who would so win it destroys it;
        He who would hold it in his grasp loses it.

        The course and nature of things is such that
            What was in front is now behind;
            What warmed anon we freezing find.
            Strength is of weakness oft the spoil;
            The store in ruins mocks our toil.

        Hence the sage puts away excessive effort,
            extravagance, and easy indulgence.

29.   Nature has self-poise in all her works;
         Certain proportions in which oxygen and azote combine,
         And not less a harmony in faculties,
            a fitness in the spring and the regulator.

         So let man be,
         Let him empty his breast of his windy conceits
         And show his lordship by manners and deeds
            on the scale of nature.

         Nature, hating art and pains,
         Balks and baffles plotting brains.
         The divine circulations never rest nor linger;
         We are encamped in nature, not domesticated.

         It is firm water, it is cold flame.

30.   He who would assist a lord of men
          in harmony with the Tao
      Will not assert his mastery in the kingdom
          by force of arms.
      Such a course is sure to meet with its proper return.

      Wherever a host is stationed, briars and thorns spring up.
      In the sequence of great armies, there are sure to be bad years.

      A skillful commander strikes a decisive blow and stops.
      He does not dare to assert and complete his mastery.
      He will strike a blow, but will be on his guard
          against being vain or boastful or arrogant
          in consequence of it.
      He strikes it as a matter of necessity;
      He strikes it, but not from a wish for mastery.

      When things have attained their maturity, they become old.
      This may be said to be not in accordance with the Tao,
      And what is not in accordance with it soon comes to an end.

30.   War begins to look like an epidemic insanity,
        Breaking out here and there like the cholera
            or influenza
        Infecting men's brains.

        When seen in the remote past,
            in the infancy of society,
        Appears a part of the connection of events
            and in its place, necessary.

        War and peace thus resolve themselves
            into a mercury of the state of cultivation.
        At certain stages, the man fights,
            if he be of sound body and mind.
        At a certain higher stage,
            he makes no offensive demonstration.
        His warlike nature is all concerted into
            an active medicinal principle.

31.   *Now arms, however beautiful,*
       are instruments of evil omen,
    Hateful, it may be said, to all creatures.
    Therefore they who have the Tao do not like to employ them.

    The superior man ordinarily considers the left hand
       the most honorable place,
    But in time of war the right hand.
    Those sharp weapons are instruments of evil omen,
       and not the instruments of the superior man—
    He uses them only on the compulsion of necessity.
    Calm and repose are what he prizes;
    Victory by force of arms is to him undesirable.
    To consider this desirable would be to delight
       in the slaughter of men;
    And he who delights in the slaughter of men
       cannot get his will in the kingdom.

    He who has killed multitudes of men
    Should weep for them with the bitterest grief.

31.   The instinct of self-help is very early unfolded
          in the coarse and merely brute form of war.
      To men of a sedate and mature spirit,
          in whom is any knowledge or mental activity,
      The detail of battle becomes unsupportably
          tedious and revolting.
      Nothing is plainer than that the sympathy
          with war
      Is a juvenile and temporary state.
      The standing army, the arsenal, the camp
          and the gibbet
      Do not appertain to man.
      They only serve as an index to show
          where man is now;
      What a bad, unorganized temper he has;
      What an ugly neighbor he is; how low his hope lies.

      Cannot love be, as well as hate?
      Cannot peace be, as well as war?

32.   *The Tao, considered as unchanging, has no name.*

Though in its primordial simplicity, it may be small,
The whole world dares not deal with it as a minister.
If a feudal prince or king could guard and hold it,
All would spontaneously submit themselves to him.
Heaven and earth, under its guidance, unite together
    and send down the sweet dew,
Which, without the directions of men,
    reaches equally everywhere as of its own accord.
As soon as it proceeds to action, it has a name.
When it once has that name,
Men can know to rest in it.
When they know to rest in it,
They can be free from all risk of failure or error.

The relation of the Tao to all the world
    is like that of the great rivers and seas
    to the streams from the valleys.

32.   This deep power in which we rest
And whose beatitudes are all accessible to us,
Is not only self-sufficing and perfect
    in every hour;
But the act of seeing and the thing seen,
The seer and the spectacle,
The subject and the object,
        are one.

Nature judges like a God all men that
    come to her.
That power, which does not respect quantity,
Which makes the whole and the particle
    its equal channel,
Delegates its smile to the morning,
And distills its essence into every drop of rain.

33.   *He who knows other men is discerning;*
        He who knows himself is intelligent.
        He who overcomes others is strong;
        He who overcomes himself is mighty.

        He who is satisfied with his lot is rich;
        He who goes on acting with energy has a firm will.
        He who does not fail in the requirements of his position,
            continues long;
        He who dies and yet does not perish, has longevity.

33.   He who knows that power is inborn,
That he is weak because he has looked
    for good out of him,
    and elsewhere,
And so perceiving, throws himself
    unhesitatingly on his thoughts,
Instantly rights himself, stands in
    the erect position,
Commands his limbs, works miracles,
Just as a man who stands on his feet
    is stronger than a man who stands on his head.

34.　　　*All-pervading is the great Tao!*
It may be found on the left hand
　　　and on the right.
All things depend on it for their production,
Which it gives to them, not one refusing obedience to it.
When its work is accomplished,
　　　it does not claim the name of having done it.
It clothes all things as with a garment,
And makes no assumption of being their lord—
It may be named in the smallest things.
All things return to their root and disappear,
And do not know that it is it which presides
　　　over their doing so—
It may be named in the greatest things.

Hence the sage is able in the same way
　　　to accomplish his great achievements.
It is through his not making himself great
　　　that he can accomplish them.

34.　　For wisdom is infused into every form;
　　　　The divine circulations never rest or linger.
　　　　The dance of the hours goes forward still;
　　　　　　like an odor of incense, like a strain of music,
　　　　　　like sleep,
　　　　It is inexact and boundless.

　　　　This energy comes to the lowly and simple.
　　　　It comes to whomever will put off
　　　　　　what is foreign and proud;
　　　　It comes as insight; it comes as serenity
　　　　　　and grandeur.

35. To him who holds in his hand the Great Image
          of the Invisible Tao,
     The whole world repairs.
     Men resort to him, and receive no hurt,
     But find rest, peace, and the feeling of ease.

     Music and dainties will make the passing guest
          stop for a time.
     But though the Tao, as it comes from the mouth,
          seems insipid and has no flavor,
     Though it seems not worth being looked at
          or listened to,
     The use of it is inexhaustible.

35. He is great who is what he is from nature,
        and never reminds us of this.
    The world is upheld by the veracity of good men.
    They make the earth wholesome.

    We value total powers and effects,
        as the spirit or quality of the man.
    We have another sight, and a new standard,
    An insight which disregards what is done for the eye;
    An ear which hears not what men say
        but what they do not say.

36.   *When one is about to take an inspiration,*
          he is sure to make a previous expiration;
       When he is going to weaken another,
          he will first strengthen him;
       When he is going to overthrow another,
          he will first have raised him up;
       When he is going to despoil another,
          he will first have made gifts to him—
       This is called "hiding the light of his procedure."

       The soft overcomes the hard;
       And the weak, the strong.

       Fishes should not be taken from the deep;
       Instruments for the profit of a state
          should not be shown to the people.

36.   Polarity, or action and reaction, we meet
            in every part of nature;
        In the inspiration and expiration of
            plants and animals;
        A surplusage given to one part
            is paid out of a reduction from another part.
        What we gain in power is lost in time.
        Every sweet hath its sour;
        every evil its good.
        For everything you gain, you lose something.

        There is always some leveling circumstance
            that puts down the overbearing, the strong.

37.   *The Tao in its regular course does nothing*
           for the sake of doing it,
       And so there is nothing which it does not do.

       If princes and kings were able to maintain it,
       All things would of themselves
       Be transformed by them.

       If this transformation became to me
           an object of desire,
       I would express the desire by the nameless simplicity.

       Simplicity without a name
       Is free from all external aim.
       With no desire, at rest and still,
       All things go right as of their will.

37.   When a man, through stubbornness,
           insists to do this or that,
       Something absurd or whimsical,
           only because he will,
       He is weak.
       He blows with his lips against the tempest;
       He calms the incoming ocean with his cane.

       Shun passion, fold the hands of thrift,
       Sit still and truth is near;
       Suddenly, it will uplift
       Your eyelids to the sphere:
       Wait a little, you shall see.

自然
无法

Tao
follows
Nature

38.	*Those who possessed in the highest degree*
	the attributes of the Tao
Did not seek to show them,
And therefore they possessed them in fullest measure.
Those who possessed in a lower degree those attributes
Sought how not to lose them,
And therefore they did not possess them in fullest measure.

Those who possessed in the highest degree those attributes
Did nothing with a purpose, and had no need to do anything.
Those who possessed them in a lower degree
	were always doing, and had need to be so doing.

Those who possessed the highest benevolence
	were always seeking to carry it out,
	and had no need to be doing so.
Those who possessed the highest righteousness
	were always seeking to carry it out,
	and had need to be so doing.

Thus it was that when the Tao was lost,
	its attributes appeared;
When its attributes were lost, benevolence appeared;
When benevolence was lost, righteousness appeared;
And when righteousness was lost, the proprieties appeared.

Thus it is that the great man abides by what is solid,
	and eschews what is flimsy;
Dwells with the fruit and not with the flower.

38.   Men achieve a certain greatness unawares
          when working to another aim.
       They teach us the qualities of primary nature,
          admit us to the constitution of things.
       What they know, they know for us.
       With each new man a new secret of nature transpires.
       The escape from all false ties;
          courage to be what we are;
          and love of what is simple and beautiful;
       These are the essentials.

       The wise man shows his wisdom in separation,
          in gradation,
       And his scale of creatures and of merits
          is as wide as nature.
       The foolish have no range in their scale,
          but suppose every man is as every other man.
       What is not good, they call the worst,
       And what is not hateful, they call the best.

       In like manner, what good heed nature forms in us!
       She pardons no mistakes.
       Her yea is yea, her nay, nay.

       The hero is he who is immovably centered.

39. The things which from of old have got the Tao are—
        Heaven which by it is bright and pure;
        Earth rendered thereby firm and sure;
        Spirits with powers by it supplied;
        Valleys kept full throughout their void;
        All creatures which through it do live;
        Princes and kings who from it get
        The model which to all they give.
  All these are the results of the Tao.

  If heaven were not thus pure, it soon would rend;
  If earth were not thus sure, 'twould break and bend;
  Without these powers, the spirits soon would fail;
  If not so filled, the drought would parch each vale;
  Without that life, creatures would pass away;
  Princes and kings, without that moral sway,
  However grand and high, would all decay.

39.   It is the universal nature, which gives worth
            to particular men and things.
        Nature is an immutable cloud, which is always
            and never the same.
        Every chemical substance, every plant,
            every animal in its growth,
        Teaches the unity of cause, the variety of appearance.

        All laws derive hence their ultimate reason;
        All express more or less distinctly some command of
            this supreme, illimitable essence.

        There is no great and no small
        To the soul that maketh all.
        And where it cometh, all things are;
        And it cometh everywhere.
        Eyes are found in light; ears in auricular air;
        Feet on land; fins in water; wings in air.
        And each creature where it was meant to be,
            with a mutual fitness.

40.   *The movement of the Tao*
         By contraries proceeds;
And weakness marks the course
     Of Tao's mighty deeds.

40.   Every natural fact is an emanation,
            and that from which it emanates
            is an emanation also,
        And from every emanation
            is a new emanation.
        A mysterious principle of life
            must be assumed,
        Which not only inhabits the organ,
            but makes the organ.

41. *Scholars of the highest class, when they hear about the Tao,*
   earnestly carry it into practice.
   Scholars of the middle class, when they have heard about it,
   seem now to keep it and now to lose it.
   Scholars of the lowest class, when they have heard about it,
   laugh greatly at it.
   If it were not thus laughed at, it would not be fit to be the Tao.

Therefore, the sentence makers have thus expressed themselves:
   The Tao, when brightest seen, seems light to lack;
   Who progress in it makes, seems drawing back;
   Its even way is like a rugged track.
   Its highest virtue from the vale doth rise;
   Its greatest beauty seems to offend the eyes:
   And he has most whose lot the least supplies.
   Its firmest virtue seems but poor and low;
   Its solid truth seems change to undergo;
   Its largest square doth yet no corner show;
   A vessel great, it is the slowest made.
   Loud is its sound, but never word it said.
   A semblance great, the shadow of a shade.

41. There is a certain wisdom of humanity
   Which is common to the greatest man with the lowest;
   The learned and studious of thought
    have no monopoly of wisdom.
   We owe many valuable observations to people
    who are not very acute or profound.
   The action of the soul is oftener in that
    which is felt and left unsaid,
   Than that which is said in any conversation.
   We know better than we do.

   That which once existed in intellect as pure law
    has now taken body as nature.
   It existed already in the mind in solution;
   Now it has been precipitated,
   And the bright sediment is the world.
   We could never surprise nature in a corner;
   It is inexact and boundless.
   Talent goes from without inward.
   When Genius arrives, it flows out of a deeper source
    than the foregoing silence.
   Here about us coils forever the agent enigma,
    so old, and so unutterable.

42.   *The Tao produced One; One produced Two;*
Two produced Three; Three produced all things.
All things leave behind them the Obscurity
    out of which they have come,
And go forward to embrace the Brightness
    into which they have emerged,
While they are harmonized by the Breath of Vacancy.

What men dislike is to be orphans,
    to have little virtue, to be as carriages without naves;
And yet these are the designations which kings
    and princes use for themselves.
So it is that some things are increased by being diminished,
    and others are diminished by being increased.

What other men teach, I also teach.
The violent and strong do not die their natural death.
I will make this the basis of my teaching.

42.   The incessant movement and progress
            in which all things partake
        Could never become sensible to us but by contrast
            To some principle of fixture or stability in the soul.
        We can never be quite strangers or inferiors in nature.
        It is flesh of our flesh, and bone of our bone.

        'Tis the old secret of the gods,
        That they come in low disguises.
        'Tis the vulgar great, who come dizened
            with gold and jewels.
        Real kings hide their crowns away in their wardrobes,
            and affect a plain and poor exterior.

        The real and lasting victories are those of peace,
            and not of war.
        The way to conquer the foreign artisan
            is not to kill him, but to beat his work.

43.   The softest thing in the world dashes against
            and overcomes the hardest;
        That which has no substantial existence enters
            where there is no crevice.
        I know hereby what advantage belongs
            to doing nothing with a purpose.
        There are a few in the world who attain
            to the teaching without words,
        And the advantage arising from non-action.

43.   All is riddle, and the key to a riddle
            is another riddle.
        To change and to flow, the gas becomes solid,
        And phantoms and nothings
            return to be things.
        Prudence consists in avoiding
            and going without,
        Not in the inventing of means and methods,
        Not in adroit steering, not in gentle repairing.

44.   Or fame or life,
            Which do you hold more dear?
        Or life or wealth,
            To which would you adhere?
        Keep life and lose those other things;
        Keep them and lose your life—which
            brings
        Sorrow and pain more near?

        Thus we may see
            Who cleaves to fame
        Rejects what is more great;
        Who loves large stores
            Gives up the richer state.

        Who is content
        Needs fear no shame.
        Who knows to stop
        Incurs no blame.
        From danger free
        Long live shall he.

44.   Genius consists in neither improving nor
        remembering,
But in both trembles the beam
   of the balance of nature.
Two brains in every man
Who walks in ways that are unfamed
And feats achieved before they're named.

There is a teaching for him from within
   which is leading him in a new path,
And, the more it is trusted,
Separates and signalizes him,
While it makes him more important and
   necessary to society.
So that his doing, which is perfectly natural,
Appears miraculous to dull people.

45.   *Who thinks his great achievements poor*
          Shall find his vigor long endure.
          Of greatest fullness, deemed a void,
          Exhaustion ne'er shall stem the tide.
          Do thou what's straight still crooked deem;
          Thy greatest art still stupid seem,
          And eloquence a stammering scream.

          Constant action overcomes cold;
              Being still overcomes heat.
          Purity and stillness give the correct law
              to all under heaven.

45.   The men we call greatest are least
            in this kingdom.
        He that despiseth small things
            will perish little by little.
        Let him esteem nature a perpetual counselor
            and her perfections the exact
            measure of our deviations.

        Do not craze yourself with thinking,
        But go about your business anywhere.
        Life is not intellectual or critical,
            but sturdy.

46.　　*When the Tao prevails in the world,*
They send back their swift horses to draw
　　the dung-carts.
When the Tao is disregarded in the world,
The warhorses breed in the borderlands.

There is no guilt greater than to sanction ambition;
No calamity greater than to be discontented
　　with one's lot;
No fault greater than the wish to be getting.
Therefore, the sufficiency of contentment is an enduring
　　and unchanging sufficiency.

46. A man's wisdom is to know that
         all ends are momentary.
     If he listens with insatiable ears,
         richer and greater wisdom is taught him.
     He is the fool of ideas and leads a heavenly life.
     His health and greatness consists
         in his being the channel through which
         heaven flows to earth.
     What man, seeing this, can lose it
         from his thoughts.

47. *Without going outside his door, one understands*
      all that takes place under the sky;
   Without looking out from his window, one sees
      the Tao of Heaven.
   The farther that one goes out from himself,
      the less he knows.

   Therefore the sages got their knowledge
      without traveling;
   Gave their right name to things without seeing them;
   And accomplished their ends without any purpose
      of doing so.

47.   The soul is no traveler;
        The wise man stays at home.
        He does not go abroad with the hope of finding
            somewhat greater than he knows.
        The soul that is plain and true
            dwells in the hour that now is,
            in the earnest experience of the common day,
        And the mere trifle becomes porous to thought,
            and bibulous to the sea of light.

48. *He who devotes himself to learning seeks*
 from day to day to increase his knowledge;
He who devotes himself to the Tao seeks
 from day to day to diminish his doing.
He diminishes it and again diminishes it,
 till he arrives at doing nothing (on purpose).
Having arrived at this point of non-action, there is
 nothing which he does not do.

48.   Let us unlearn our wisdom of the world.
       Let us take our bloated nothingness out of
           the path of divine circuits.
       Let us lie low and learn that truth alone
           makes rich and great.
       The rich mind lies in the sun and sleeps,
           and is nature.
       To think is to act.

49.   *The sage has no invariable mind of his own;*
        He makes the mind of the people his mind.

        To those who are good to me, I am good;
        And to those who are not good to me,
            I am also good—
        And thus, all get to be good.
        To those who are sincere with me,
            I am sincere;
        And to those who are not sincere with me,
            I am also sincere—
        And thus all get to be sincere.

        The sage has in the world an appearance
            of indecision,
        And keeps his mind in a state of indifference to all.
        The people all keep their eyes and ears directed to him,
            and he deals with them all as his children.

49. By the permanence of nature, minds are trained alike
        and made intelligible to each other.
    Good and bad are but names very readily
        transferable to that or this.
    I ought to go upright and vital
        and speak the rude truth in all ways.
    My life is for itself and not for spectacle.

    The great man is he who in the midst of the crowd
    Keeps with perfect sweetness
        the independence of solitude.
    The wise man shall make men sensible
        by the expression of his countenance,
    That he goes the missionary of wisdom and virtue.

50.   *Men come forth and live; they enter again and die.*

Of every ten, three are ministers of life;
And three are ministers of death.
There are also three in every ten
   whose aim is to live,
      but whose movements tend to the land of death.
And for what reason?
Because of their excessive endeavors to perpetuate life.

But I have heard that he who is skillful
   at managing the life entrusted to him
For a time travels on the land
   without having to shun rhinoceros or tiger,
And enters a host without having to avoid
   buff coat or sharp weapon.
The rhinoceros finds no place in him
   into which to thrust its horn,
Nor the tiger a place in which to fix its claws,
Nor the weapon a place to admit its point.
And for what reason?
Because there is in him no place of death.

50.   The name of death was never terrible
       to him that knew to live.
    A man of thought is willing to die,
       willing to live.

    The world is delivered into your hand,
       but on two conditions—
    Not for property, but for use,
    Use according to the noble nature of the gift,
       not for toys, and not for self-indulgence.
    Things work to their ends, not yours,
    And will certainly defeat any adventurer
       who fights against this ordination.

    On the borders of the grave, the wise man
       looks forward with elasticity of mind, or hope.

51.   *All things are produced by the Tao,*
        and nourished by its outflowing operation.
      They receive their forms according to the nature of each,
        and are completed according
        to the circumstances of their condition.
      Therefore all things without exception
        honor the Tao,
      And exalt its outflowing operation.
      Thus it is that the Tao produces all things,
      Nourishes them, brings them to their full growth,
      Nurses them, completes them, matures them,
        maintains them, and overspreads them.

      It produces them and makes no claim
        to the possession of them;
      It carries them through their processes
        and does not vaunt its ability in doing so;
      It brings them to maturity and exercises
        no control over them—
      This is called its mysterious operation.

51.   The method of nature: who could ever analyze it?
      The simplicity of nature is not that
         which may be easily read,
      But it is inexhaustible.
      The spirit and peculiarity of that impression is
      That it does not exist to any one or to any number
         of particular hands,
      But to numberless and endless benefit.
      There is in it no private will, no rebel leaf or limb,
         but the whole is oppressed by
         our superincumbent tendency.

      Nature converts itself into a vast promise,
         and will not be rashly explained.

52.   The Tao which originated all under the sky
      Is to be considered as the mother of them all.

      When the mother is found,
      We know what her children should be.
      When one knows that he is his mother's child,
          and proceeds to guard the mother that belongs to him,
      To the end of his life he will be free from all peril.

      Let him keep his mouth closed, and shut up
          the portals of his nostrils,
      And all his life he will be exempt from laborious exertion.
      Let him keep his mouth opened,
          and spend his breath
          in the promotion of his affairs,
      And all his life there will be no safety for him.

      The perception of what is small is the secret
          of clear-sightedness;
      The guarding of what is soft and tender
          is the secret of strength.

      Who uses well his light,
      Reverting to its source so bright,
      Will from his body ward all blight,
      And hides the unchanging from men's sight.

52.   Under all this running sea of circumstance,
      whose waters ebb and flow with perfect balance,
      lies the aboriginal abyss of real Being.
Let me see every trifle bristling with
      the polarity that ranges it instantly
      on an internal law.
And the shop, the plough, and the ledger
      refer to the like cause by which
      light undulates and poets sing.
The world lies no longer a dull miscellany,
      but has form and order;
There is no trifle, there is no puzzle;
But one design writes and animates
      the farthest pinnacle and the lowest trench.

There is always life for the living;
      What a man has done a man can do.
      Every man is provided with a key to nature,
      And that man only rightly knows himself
      as far as he has experimented on things.

53.   If I were suddenly to become known,
        And put in a position to conduct
            a government according to the great Tao,
        What I should be most afraid of would be a boastful display.

        The great Tao is very level and easy;
            But people love the byways.

        Their courtyards and buildings shall be well kept,
        But their fields shall be ill cultivated,
            and their granaries very empty.
        They shall wear elegant and ornamented robes,
            carry a sharp sword at their girdle,
            pamper themselves in eating and drinking,
            and have a superabundance of property and wealth—
        Such princes may be called robbers and boasters.
        This is contrary to the Tao surely!

53.   What a man does, that he has.
        Let him regard no good as solid,
           but that which is in his nature.
        The goods of fortune may come and go
           like summer leaves;
        Let him scatter them on every wind
           as momentary signs.

        Virtue is the adherence in action
           to the nature of things,
        And the nature of things makes it prevalent.
        It consists in a perpetual substitution
           of being for seeming.

        Why need you choose so painfully your place,
           and occupation, and association and modes of action?
        For you, there is a reality, a fit place
           and congenial duties.

54.   *What Tao's skillful planter plants*
           Can never be uptorn;
What his skillful arms enfold,
           From him can ne'er be borne.
Sons shall bring in lengthening line,
Sacrifices to his shrine.

Tao, when nursed within one's self,
           His vigor will make true;
And where the family it rules
           What riches will accrue!
The neighborhood where it prevails
           In thriving will abound;
And when 'tis seen throughout the state,
           Good fortune will be found.
Employ it in the kingdom o'er
           And men thrive all around.

54.   All power is of one kind.
        The mind that is parallel with the laws of nature
        Will be in the current of events and strong
            with their strength.

        Who has learned to root himself in being,
            and wholly to cease from seeming,
        He is domestic, and he is at the heart of nature.

        Concentration is the secret of strength.
        The importance of one person who has the truth
            over nations who have it not,
        Is because power obeys reality, and not appearance,
            according to quality, and not quantity.

55.   He who has in himself abundantly
          the attributes of the Tao is like an infant.
       Poisonous insects will not sting him;
       Fierce beasts will not seize him;
       Birds of prey will not strike him.

       The infant's bones are weak
       And its sinews soft, but yet its grasp is firm.
       It knows not yet the union of male and female,
       And yet its virile member may be excited—
          showing the perfection of its physical essence.
       All day long it will cry out without becoming hoarse—
          showing the harmony in its constitution.

       To him by whom this harmony is known,
       The secret of the unchanging Tao is shown,
       And in the knowledge wisdom finds its throne.
       All life-increasing arts to evil turn;
       Where the mind makes the vital breath to burn,
       False is the strength, and o'er it we should mourn.

       When things have become strong,
       They then become old,
       Which may be said to be contrary to the Tao.
       Whatever is contrary to the Tao soon ends.

55. The will constitutes the man.
    He has his life in nature, like a beast,
    But choice is born in him;
    He chooses as the rest of creation does not.

    But will, pure and perceiving, is not willfulness.

    The high, contemplative, all-commanding vision,
        the sense of Right and Wrong, is alike in all.
    Its attributes are self-existence, eternity,
        intuition, and command.
    It is the mind of the mind.
    We belong to it, not it to us.

    Whilst a man seek good ends,
    He is strong by the whole strength of nature.
    Insofar as he roves from these ends,
    He bereaves himself of power,
    He becomes less and less.

56.　　He who knows the Tao does not care to speak about it;
　　　　He who is ever ready to speak about it does not know it.

　　　　He who knows it will keep his mouth shut
　　　　　　and close the portals of his nostrils.
　　　　He will blunt his sharp points
　　　　　　and unravel the complications of things;
　　　　He will temper his brightness, and bring himself
　　　　　　into agreement with the obscurity of others.
　　　　This is called the mysterious agreement.

　　　　Such a one cannot be treated familiarly
　　　　　　or distantly;
　　　　He is beyond all consideration of profit
　　　　　　or injury;
　　　　Of nobility or meanness—
　　　　He is the noblest man under heaven.

56.   He that thinks most will say the least.

The less a man thinks or knows about his virtues,
    the better we like him.

To finish the moment, he finds the journey's end
    in every step of the road;
To him, the greatest number of good hours is wisdom.

For it is only the finite that has wrought
    and suffered;
The infinite lies stretched in smiling repose.

57.   *A state may be ruled by measures of correction;*
        Weapons of war may be used with crafty dexterity;
        But the kingdom is made one's own
            only by freedom from action and purpose.

        How do I know that it is so? By these facts—
        In the kingdom, the multiplication of prohibitive enactments
            increases the poverty of the people;
        The more implements to add to their profit that the people have,
            the greater disorder is there in the state and clan;
        The more acts of crafty dexterity that men possess,
            the more do strange contrivances appear;
        The more display there is of legislation,
            the more thieves and robbers there are.

        Therefore, a sage has said, "I will do nothing of purpose,
            and the people will be transformed of themselves.
        I will be fond of keeping still,
            and the people will of themselves become correct.
        I will take the trouble about it,
            and the people will themselves become rich;
        I will manifest no ambition,
            and the people will of themselves attain
            to the primitive simplicity."

57.   We live in a very low state of the world
          and pay unwilling tribute to governments
          founded in force.

      The tendencies of the times favor
          the idea of self-government
      And leave the individual, for all code,
          to the rewards and penalties of his own constitution.

      Therefore, all public ends look vague and quixotic
          beside private ones.
      For any laws but those which men
          make for themselves are laughable.

      Hence, the less government we have the better,
          the fewer laws, and the less confided power.
      The power of love, as the basis of the state,
          has never been tried.

      We must not imagine that all things
          are lapsing into confusion,
      If every tender protestant be not compelled
          to bear his part in certain social conventions:
      Nor doubt that roads can be built,
      Letters carried, and the fruit of laborers secured
          when the government of force is at hand.
      Could not a nation of friends devise a better way?

58.   The government that seems the most unwise,
      Oft goodness to the people best supplies;
      That which is meddling, touching everything,
      Will work but ill, and disappointment bring.

      Misery!—happiness is to be found by its side!
      Happiness!—misery lurks beneath it!
      Who knows what either will come to in the end?

      Shall we then dispense with correction?
      The method of correction shall by a turn
          become distortion,
      And the good in it shall by a turn become evil.
      The delusion of the people on this point
          has indeed subsisted for a long time.

      Therefore the sage is like a square,
      Which cuts no one with its angles;
      Like a corner, which injures no one with its sharpness.
      He is straightforward, but allows himself no license;
      He is bright, but does not dazzle.

58. Our time is too full of activity and performance.
The world is governed too much;
Things have their laws, as well as man;
   and refuse to be trifled with.

In changing moon, in tidal wave,
Glows the feud of Want and Have,
Mountain tall and ocean deep
Trembling balance duly keep.

An inevitable dualism bisects nature.
The reaction, so grand in the elements,
   is repeated within small boundaries.
Every excess causes a defect;
Every defect an excess.
Every sweet hath its sour, every evil its good.

A wise man will extend this lesson
   to all parts of life;
When he is pushed, tormented, defeated,
He has a chance to learn something,
   is cured of the insanity of conceit,
    has got moderation and real skill.

59.   *For regulating the human and rendering service to the heavenly,*
          there is nothing like moderation.

It is only by this moderation that there is effected
    an early return to man's normal state.
That early return is what I call the repeated accumulation
    of the attributes of the Tao.
With that repeated accumulation of those attributes, there comes
    a subjugation of every obstacle to such return.
Of this subjugation we know not what shall be the limit;
And when one knows not what the limit shall be,
    he may be the ruler of a state.

He who possesses the mother of the state may continue long.
His case is like that of the plant, of which we say
    that its roots are deep and its flower stalks firm—
This is the way to secure that its enduring life
    shall long be seen.

59.   By your own act you teach the beholder
           how to do the practicable.
       According to the depth from which you draw
           your life,
       Such is the depth not only of your strenuous effort,
           but of your manners and presence.
       Leave the military hurry and adopt the pace of nature.
       Her secret is patience.
       Have the self-command you wish to inspire.
       Your teaching and discipline must have
           the reserve and taciturnity of nature.
       Say little; do not snarl; do not chide;
           but govern by the eye.
       See what they need and the right thing is done.

60. *Governing a great state is like cooking small fish.*

Let the kingdom be governed according to the Tao,
And the manes of the departed will not manifest
    their spiritual energy.
It is not that those manes have not that spiritual energy,
    but it will not be employed to hurt men.
It is not that it could not hurt men,
    but neither does the ruling sage hurt them.

When these two do not injuriously affect each other,
Their good influences converge in the virtue of the Tao.

60.   Fear, Craft and Avarice
            cannot rear a state;
        The more reason, the less government.
        In a sensible family, nobody hears
            the words "shall" and "shan't."
        Nobody commands and nobody obeys
            but all conspire and joyfully cooperate.
        The wise know that foolish legislation
            is a rope of sand
            which perishes in the twisting.
        The law is only a memorandum.

        When the statehouse is the hearth,
            the perfect state is come.

61.   *What makes a great state is its being like a low-lying,*
           down-flowing stream—
      It becomes the center to which tend all
           the small states under heaven.

      To illustrate from the case of all females—
      The female always overcomes the male by her stillness.
      Stillness may be considered a sort of abasement.

      Thus it is that a great state, by condescending
           to small states, gains them for itself;
      And that small states, by abasing themselves
           to a great state, win it over to them.
      In the one case the abasement leads to
           gaining adherents,
      In the other case to procuring favor.

      The great state only wishes to unite men together
           and nourish them;
      A small state only wishes to be received by, and to serve, the other.
      Each gets what it desires,
           but the great state must learn to abase itself.

61.   The excellence of men consists
            in the completeness with which
            the lower system is taken up into the higher—
       A process of much time and delicacy.

       Those who are capable of humility, of justice,
            of love, of aspiration,
       Stand already on a platform that commands
            action and grace.

       This is the law of moral and mental gain.
       The simplest rise as by specific levity,
            not into a particular virtue,
       But into the region of all virtues.

       Sympathy, the female force, is more subtle, and lasting,
            and creative.

62.   *Tao has of all things the most honored place.*
No treasures give good men so rich a grace;
Bad men it guards and doth their ill efface.

Its admirable words can purchase honor;
Its admirable deeds can raise their performer above others.
Even men who are not good are not abandoned by it.

Why was it that the ancients prized this Tao so much?
Was it not because it could be got by seeking for it,
And the guilty could escape from the stain of their guilt by it?
This is the reason why all under heaven consider it
        the most valuable thing.

62.   With a geometry of sunbeams, the soul
            lays the foundation of nature.
        Of this pure nature, every man is at some time sensible.
        Language cannot paint it with its colors.
        It is too subtle, it is indefinable,
            unmeasurable,
        But we know that it pervades and contains us.

        The truth and grandeur of this thought
            is proved by its scope and applicability,
        For it commands the entire schedule
            and inventory of things for its illustration.

63.   *It is the way of the Tao to act*
          without thinking of acting;
      To conduct affairs without feeling
          the trouble of them;
      To taste without discerning any flavor;
      To consider what is small as great,
          and a few as many;
      And to recompense injury with kindness.

      The master of it anticipates things that are difficult
          while they are easy,
      And does things that would become great
          while they are small.
      All difficult things in the world are sure to arise
          from a previous state in which they were easy,
      And all great things from one in which they were small.

      He who lightly promises is sure to keep
          but little faith;
      He who is continually thinking things easy
          is sure to find them difficult.
      Therefore the sage sees difficulty
          even in what seems easy,
      And so never has any difficulties.

63.   Clinging to nature, or that province of nature
           which he knows,
       He makes no mistake, but works after her laws,
           and at her own pace.
       That man will go far—
       For you see in his manners
           that recognition of him by others is
           not necessary to him.
       So that his doing, which is perfectly natural,
           appears miraculous.

       A sensible man does not brag,
       Omits himself as habitually
           as another man obtrudes himself in the discourse.

64. *That which is at rest is easily kept hold of;*
Before a thing has given indications of its presence,
*   it is easy to take measures against it;*
That which is brittle is easily broken;
That which is very small is easily dispersed.
Action should be taken before a thing
*   has made its appearance;*
Order should be secured before disorder has begun.

The tree which fills the arms grew
*   from the tiniest sprout;*
The tower of nine stories rose from a small heap of earth;
The journey of a thousand li
*   commenced with a single step.*

He who acts with an ulterior purpose does harm;
He who takes hold of a thing in the same way
*   loses his hold.*
The sage does not act so,
*   and therefore does no harm;*
He does not lay hold so,
*   and therefore does not lose his hold.*

The sage desires what other men do not desire,
*   and does not prize things difficult to get;*
He learns what other men do not learn, and turns back
*   to what the multitude of men have passed by.*
Thus he helps the natural development of all things,
And does not dare to act with an ulterior purpose of his own.

64.   Every ultimate fact is only the first
         of a new series.
      There is no outside, no inclosing wall,
         no circumference to us.
      That which builds is better than
         that which is built.
      Cause and effect, means and ends, seed and fruit
         cannot be severed;
      For the effect already blooms in the cause,
      The end preexists in the means,
      The fruit is in the seed.

      Our strength grows our weakness;
      Whilst a man sits on the cushion of advantages,
         he goes to sleep.

      The man who renounces himself,
         comes to himself.
      Every step so downward, is a step upward.
      Words and actions are not the attributes of
         a brute nature;
      They cannot cover the dimensions of
         what is in truth.
      The wise man, in doing one thing, does all;
      Or, in the one thing he does rightly,
      He sees the likeness of all which is done rightly.

65.   The ancients who showed their skill in practicing the Tao
            did so not to enlighten the people,
        But rather to make them simple and ignorant.

        The difficulty in governing the people arises
            from their having much knowledge.
        Who tries to govern the state by his wisdom
            is a scourge to it;
        While he who does not try to do so is a blessing.

        He who knows these two things finds in them
            also his model and rule.
        Ability to know this model and rule constitutes what we call
            the mysterious excellence of a governor.
        Deep and far-reaching is such mysterious excellence,
        Showing indeed its possessor as opposite to others,
        But leading them to a great conformity to him.

65.   As fast as the public mind is opened
        to more intelligence,
The code is seen to be brute and stammering.

The wise know that the State must follow and not lead
    the character and progress of the citizen.
The strongest usurper is quickly got rid of,
And that form of government which prevails
Is the expression of what cultivation exists
    in the population which permits it.

The history of the State sketches in coarse outline
    the progress of thought.
And follows at a distance the delicacy
    of culture and aspiration.

66. That whereby the rivers and seas are able to receive
the homage and tribute of all the valley streams,
is their skill in being lower than they—
It is thus that they are the kings of them all.
So it is that the sage, wishing to be above men,
puts himself by his words below them,
And wishing to be before them, places his person behind them.

66.   A sensible man avoids introducing the names
            of his creditable companions,
        And is content putting his fact or theme
            simply on its ground.
        You shall not tell me that your commercial house,
            your partners or yourself are of importance;
        You shall not tell me that you have learned
            to know men;
        You shall make me feel that
            your saying so unsays it.

67.   All the world says that, while my Tao is great,
It yet appears to be inferior to other systems of teaching.
Now it is just its greatness that makes it seem to be inferior.
If it were like any other system,
    for long would its smallness have been known!

With gentleness I can be bold;
With economy I can be liberal;
Shrinking from taking precedence of others,
    I can become a vessel of the highest honor.
Nowadays they give up gentleness
    and are all for being bold;
Economy, and are all for being liberal;
The hindmost place, and seek only to be foremost;
    of all which the end is death.

Gentleness is sure to be victorious even in battle,
    and firmly to maintain its ground.
Heaven will save its possessor,
    by his very gentleness protecting him.

67.   Self-trust is the first secret of success.
I fear the popular notion of success
    stands in direct opposition on all points
    to the real and wholesome success.
One adores public opinion, the other private opinion,
    one fame, the other desert;
    one feats, the other humility;
    one lucre, the other love.

What is especially true of love,
    is that it is a state of extreme impressionability;
The lover has more senses and finer senses than others,
His eye and ear are telegraphs;
He reads omens on the flower, and cloud,
    and face, and gesture,
And reads them right.

68.　He who in Tao's wars has skill
　　　Assumes no martial port;
　　He who fights with most good will
　　　To rage makes no resort.
　　He who vanquishes yet still
　　　Keeps from his foes apart;
　　He whose behests men most fulfill
　　　Yet humbly plies his art.

　　Thus we say, "He ne'er contends,
　　　And therein is his might."
　　Thus we say, "Men's wills he bends,
　　　That they with him unite."
　　Thus we say, "Like Heaven's his ends,
　　　No sage of old more bright."

68.　　It is a vulgar error to suppose that
　　　　　a man must be ready to fight.
　　　　The utmost that can be demanded of the man
　　　　　is that he is incapable of a lie.
　　　　You may spit upon him; nothing could
　　　　　induce him to spit upon you—
　　　　No praises, no possessions, no compulsion
　　　　　of public opinion.
　　　　You may kick him; he will think it
　　　　　the kick of a brute,
　　　　　and will not kick you in return,
　　　　But neither your knife, nor pistol
　　　　　will ever make the slightest impression.

69.   A master of the art of war has said,
        "I do not dare to be the host (to commence the war);
        I prefer to be the guest (to act on the defensive).
        I do not dare to advance an inch;
        I prefer to retire a foot."
        This is called marshaling the ranks when there are no ranks;
        Baring the arms to fight when there are no arms to bare;
        Grasping the weapon when there is no weapon to grasp;
        Advancing against the enemy when there is no enemy.

        There is no calamity greater than lightly engaging in war.
        To do that is near losing the gentleness which is so precious.
        Thus it is that when opposing weapons are actually crossed,
                he who deplores the situation conquers.

69.   He who loves the bristle of bayonets
         only sees in their glitter
         what beforehand he feels in his heart.

The least change in the man will change
   his circumstances;
The least enlargement of his ideas,
The least mitigation of his feelings
   in respect to other men.
If, for example, he could be inspired
   with a tender kindness to the souls of men,
And should come to feel that every man was another self,
   with whom he might come to join—
Every degree of the ascendancy of this feeling
   would cause the most striking of changes of external things.

70.   My words are very easy to know and easy to practice;
      But there is no one in the world
          who is able to know and able to practice them.

      There is an originating and all-comprehending
          principle in my words,
      And an authoritative law for the things
          which I enforce.
      It is because they do not know these,
          that men do not know me.

      They who know me are few,
      And I am on that account to be prized.
      It is thus that the sage wears a poor garment
          of haircloth,
      While he carries his signet of jade in his bosom.

70.   My willful actions and acquisitions
           are but roving;
       The idlest reverie, the faintest native emotion
           commands my curiosity.
       My perception is as much a fact as the sun.

       Whenever a mind is simple
           and receives a divine wisdom,
       Old things pass away—
       Means, teachers, texts, temples fall.

       A man cannot be happy and strong
           until he, too, lives
               with nature, in the present, above time.

71.   To know and yet think we do not know
            is the highest attainment;
        Not to know and yet think we do know
            is a disease.

        It is simply by being pained at the thought
            of having this disease
            that we are preserved from it.
        The sage has not the disease.
        He knows the pain that would be
            inseparable from it;
        And therefore he does not have it.

71.   If any of us knew what we were doing,
           or where we are going,
       Then when we think we best know!
       We glide through nature and should not know
           our place again.

       All things swim and glitter;
       Our life is not so much threatened as
           our perception.

       But in the solitude to which every man
           is always returning,
       He has a sanity and revelations,
           which in his passage into new worlds
           he will carry with him.

72.   *When the people do not fear what*
            they ought to fear,
        That which is their greatest dread
            will come to them.

        Let them not thoughtlessly indulge themselves
            in their ordinary life;
        Let them not act as if weary of what
            life depends on.

        It is by avoiding such indulgence that
            such weariness does not arise.

        Therefore the sage knows these things,
            but does not parade his knowledge;
        Loves, but does not appear to set a value
            on himself.
        And thus he puts the latter alternative away
            and makes a choice of the former.

72.   The use of the world is that man may
             learn its laws.
       When a man stupid becomes a man inspired,
       When one and the same man
       Passes out of the torpid into the perceiving state,
       Leaves the din of trifles, the stupor of the senses,
             to enter into the quasi-omniscience of higher thought—
       Up and down, all around go,
       All limits disappear,
       No horizon shuts down.
       He sees things in their causes,
             all facts in their connection.

73. *He whose boldness appears in his daring*
      to do wrong, in defiance of the laws,
      is put to death;
He whose boldness in his not daring to do so,
      lives on.
Of these two cases the one appears to be
      advantageous, and the other to be injurious.

But
      When Heaven's anger smites a man,
      Who the cause shall truly scan?
On this account the sage feels a difficulty
      as to what to do in the former case.

It is the way of Heaven not to strive,
      and yet it skillfully overcomes;
Not to speak, and yet it is skillful
      in obtaining a reply;
Not to call, and yet men come to it of themselves.
Its demonstrations are quiet,
And yet its plans are skillful and effective.
The meshes of the net of Heaven are large;
Far apart, but letting nothing escape.

73.   Crime and punishment grow out of one stem.
        Punishment is a fruit that unsuspected ripens
            within the flower of the pleasure which concealed it.
        Every act rewards itself, integrates itself
            in a two-fold manner;
        First in the thing, or in real nature,
        And secondly in the circumstance,
            or apparent nature.
        The causal retribution is in the thing,
            and is seen by the soul.
        The retribution of the circumstance
            is seen by the understanding.

        What we call retribution is the universal necessity
            by which the whole appears whenever a part appears.

74.   *The people do not fear death;*
        To what purpose is it to try to frighten them with death?
        If the people were always in awe of death,
        And I could always seize those who do wrong,
            and put them to death,
        Who would dare to do wrong?

        There is always One who presides over
            the infliction of death.
        He who would inflict death in the room of him
            who so presides over it
        May be described as hewing wood
            instead of a great carpenter.
        Seldom is it that he who undertakes the hewing,
            instead of the great carpenter,
        Does not cut his own hands!

74.   Why are the masses, from the dawn of
          history down,
      Food for knives and powder?
      The idea dignified a few leaders,
          who made war and death sacred,
      But what for the wretches
          whom they hire and kill?
      The cheapness of man is every day's tragedy.

      It is a doctrine alike of the oldest,
          and of the newest philosophy,
      That man is one, and that you cannot
          injure any member
      Without a sympathetic injury
          to all the members.

75.　　*The people suffer from famine because*
　　　　　　of the multitude of taxes consumed by their superiors.
　　　　It is through this that they suffer famine.

　　　　The people are difficult to govern because
　　　　　　of the excessive agency of their superiors.
　　　　It is through this that they are difficult to govern.

　　　　The people make light of dying because
　　　　　　of the greatness of their labors
　　　　　　in seeking for the means of living.
　　　　It is this which makes them think light of dying.
　　　　Thus it is that to leave the subject of living
　　　　　　altogether out of view
　　　　Is better than to set a high value on it.

75.   The whole institution of property on its present tenures
            is injurious, and its influence on persons
            deteriorating and degrading;
        Truly, the only interest for the consideration of the state
            is persons;
        Property will always follow persons.
        The highest end of government is the culture of men.
        If men could be educated, the institutions will
            share their improvement,
        And the moral sentiment will write the law of the land.

76. *Man at his birth is supple and weak;*
    at his death, firm and strong.
So it is with all things.
Trees and plants, in their early growth,
    are soft and brittle;
At their death, dry and withered.

Thus it is that firmness and strength are
    the concomitants of death;
Softness and weakness, the concomitants of life.
Hence, he who relies on the strength of his forces
    does not conquer;
And a tree which is strong will fill the outstretched arms,
    and thereby invites the feller.

Therefore the place of what is firm and strong is below,
And that of what is soft and weak is above.

76.   When we come into the world
        A wonderful whisper gives us a direction
            for the whole road.

        Ah! If one could keep this sensibility,
            and live in the happy, sufficing present,
        And find the day and his chief means contenting,
            which only ask receptivity in you,
            and no strained exertion or cankering ambition.

        We are not strong by our power to penetrate,
            to have distinction and laurels and consumption;
        The world is enlarged for us not by new objects,
        But by finding more affinities and potencies
            than those we have.

77.   *May not the Tao of Heaven be compared*
          to the method of bending a bow?
       The part of the bow which was high is brought low,
       And what was low is raised up.
       So Heaven diminishes where there is superabundance,
          and supplements where there is deficiency.

       It is the Way of Heaven to diminish superabundance,
          and to supplement deficiency.
       It is not so with the way of man.
       He takes away from those who have not enough
          to add to his own superabundance.

       Who can take his own superabundance and
          therewith serve all under Heaven?
       Only he who is in possession of the Tao!

77.   I am born into the great, the universal mind.
       I, the imperfect, adore my own Perfect.
       I am somehow receptive of the great soul,
       And thereby do I overlook the sun and stars.
       More and more the surges of everlasting nature
           enter into me.

       I am willing also to be as passive
           to the great forces I acknowledge,
           as the thermometer, or the clock,
       And quite part with all will as superfluous.
       I am a willow of the wilderness,
           loving the wind that bent me.

78.   *There is nothing in the world more soft*
          and weak than water,
      And yet for attacking things that are firm and strong
          there is nothing that can take precedence of it—
      For there is nothing for which it can be changed.

      Everyone in the world knows that the soft
          overcomes the hard, and the weak the strong,
      But no one is able to carry it out in practice.

      Therefore a sage has said,
          "He who accepts his state's reproach,
             Is hailed therefore its altars' lord;
          To him who bears men's direful woes
             They all the name of king accord."

      Words that are strictly true seem to be paradoxical.

78.　There is a principle which is the basis of things.

A simple, quiet, undescribed, undescribable presence,
　is dwelling very peacefully in us.
We are not to do, but to let do;
　not to work, but to be worked upon.

We cannot disenchant, we cannot
　impoverish ourselves by obedience;
But by humility we rise, by obedience we command;
By poverty we are rich, by dying we live.

These facts have always suggested to man
　the sublime creed.

79.   When a reconciliation is effected after a great animosity,
        There is sure to be a grudge remaining
            in the mind of the one who was wrong.
        And how can this be beneficial to the other?

        Therefore, to guard against this, the sage keeps
            the left-hand portion of the record of the engagement,
        And does not insist on the speedy fulfillment of it
            by the other party.
        So, he who has the attributes of the Tao
            regards only the conditions of the engagement,
        While he who has not those attributes
            regards only the conditions favorable to himself.

        In the Way of Heaven, there is no partiality of love;
        It is always on the side of the good man.

79.   By going one step farther back in thought,
        Discordant opinions are reconciled
            by being seen as two extremes of one principle,
        And we can never go so far back as to
            preclude a still higher vision.

        When we get an advantage
        It is because our adversary has committed a fault.

        Forgive his crime, forgive his virtues, too,
        Those smaller faults, half convert to the right.

80.   *In a little state with a small population,*
       I would so order it, that,
       Though there were individuals with the abilities
           of ten or a hundred men,
       There should be no employment of them;
       I would make the people,
       While looking on death as a grievous thing,
       Yet not remove elsewhere to avoid it.

       Though they had boats and carriages,
       They should have no occasion to ride in them;
       Though they had buff coats and sharp weapons,
       They should have no occasion to don or use them.

       I would make the people return to the use
           of knotted cords instead of the written characters.

       They should think their coarse food sweet;
       Their plain clothes beautiful;
       Their poor dwellings places of rest;
       And their simple ways sources of enjoyment.
       There should be a neighboring state within sight,
       And the voices of the fowls and dogs
           should be heard all the way from it to us,
       But I would make the people to old age, even to death,
           not have any intercourse with it.

80.   To educate the wise man, the State exists;
       And with the appearance of the wise man,
           the State expires.
       The appearance of character
           makes the State unnecessary.

       The wise man needs no army, port, or navy—
       He loves men too well;
       No bribe, no feast, or palace to draw
           friends to him;
       No vantage ground, no favorable circumstance.

       He needs no library, for he has not done thinking;
       No church, for he is a prophet;
       No statute book, for he has the lawgiver;
       No road, for he is at home where he is;
       No experience, for the life of the creator
           shines through him and looks from his eyes.

       His relation to men is angelic; his memory
           is myrrh to them;
       His presence, frankincense and flowers.

81.   *Sincere words are not fine;*
        Fine words are not sincere.
        Those who are skilled in the Tao
            do not dispute about it;
        The disputatious are not skilled in it.
        Those who know the Tao are not extensively learned;
        The extensively learned do not know it.

        The sage does not accumulate for himself.
        The more that he expends for others,
        The more does he possess of his own;
        The more that he gives to others,
        The more does he have himself.

        With all the sharpness of the Way of Heaven,
            it injures not;
        With all the doing in the way of the sage
            he does not strive.

81. Let us not be the victims of words;
     They who speak have no more,—have less.
     I am explained without explaining;
     I am felt without action,
          and where I am not.

     The thing uttered in words is not therefore affirmed;
     He teaches who gives and he learns who receives;
     He is great who confers the most benefits.

     A consent to solitude and inaction,
          which proceeds out of an unwillingness
          to violate character,
     Is the century which makes the gem.

     I must act with truth, though I should never come to act,
          as you call it, with effect.
     I must consent to inaction, a patience which is grand.

EMERSON SOURCES
(Unless otherwise indicated all excerpts are taken from essays)

BIBLIOGRAPHY

Ames, Roger T. and David L. Hall. *Dao De Jing: A Philosophical Translation.* New York: Ballantine Books, 2003.

Bahm, Archie J. *Tao the King by Lao Tzu; Interpreted as Nature and Intelligence.* New York: Frederick Ungar Publishing, 1958.

Blofeld, John. *The Secret and Sublime: Taoist Mysteries and Magic.* New York: E. P. Dutton, 1973.

Brecht, Bertolt. *Poems 1913–1956.* Edited by John Willett and Ralph Manheim with the cooperation of Erich Fried. London and New York: Methuen, 1980.

Bynner, Witter. *The Way of Life According to Lao Tzu: An American Version.* 1944. New York: Capricorn Books, 1962.

Cabot, James Elliott. *A Memoir of Ralph Waldo Emerson.* 2 vols. London: Houghton Mifflin, 1897.

Chen, Ellen M. *The Tao Te Ching: A New Translation with Commentary.* St. Paul, Minn.: Paragon House, 1989.

Christy, Arthur. *The Orient in American Transcendentalism,* New York: Octagon Books, 1978.

Chungliang Al Huang. *Embrace Tiger, Return to Mountain: The Essence of Tai Ji.* 1973. Berkeley, Calif.: Celestial Arts, 1987.

_____. *Quantum Soup: A Philosophical Entertainment.* New York: E. P. Dutton, 1983.

Clarke, J. J. *The Tao of the West.* London and New York: Routledge, 2000.

Emerson, Ralph Waldo. *The Collected Works of Ralph Waldo Emerson.* Edited by Alfred R. Ferguson, Joseph Slater, Douglas Emory Wilson, et al. 12 vols. to date. Cambridge, Mass.: Harvard University Press, 1971–2003.

_____. *The Journals and Miscellaneous Notebooks of Ralph Waldo Emerson.* Edited by William A. Gilman, Ralph H. Orth, et al. 16 vols. Cambridge, Mass.: Harvard University Press, 1982–2003.

Ferguson, Andy. *Zen's Chinese Heritage: The Masters and Their Teachings.* Boston: Wisdom Publications, 2000.

Friedell, Egon. *A Cultural History of the Modern Age.* 3 vols. New York: Alfred A. Knopf, 1933.

Geldard, Richard. *The Spiritual Teachings of Ralph Waldo Emerson.* Hudson, N.Y.: Lindisfarne Press, 2001.

Gia-Fu Feng and Jane English, *Tao Te Ching [by] Lao Tzu: A New Translation.* New York: Knopf, 1972.

Groff, Richard. *Thoreau and the Prophetic Tradition.* Los Angeles: The Manas Publishing Co., 1961.

Grossman, Richard. *A Year with Emerson.* Boston: David Godine, 2003.

Henricks, Robert G. *Lao-tzu: Te-tao Ching: A New Translation Based on the Recently Discovered Ma-wang-tui Texts.* New York: The Modern Library, 1993.

Lau, D. C. *Lao Tzu: Tao Te Ching: Translated with an Introduction.* New York: Penguin, 1963.

Legge, James. *The Texts of Taoism.* Oxford: Oxford University Press, 1891.

Lin Yutang. *The Wisdom of Laotse.* New York: Random House, 1948.

_____. *The Wisdom of China and India.* New York: Random House, 1942.

Merton, Thomas. *The Way of Chuang Tzu.* New York: New Directions, 1965.

Mitchell, Stephen. *Tao te Ching: A New English Version.* New York: Harper & Row, 1988.

Paramananda, Swami. *Emerson and Vedanta.* 1918. Boston: The Vedanta Center, 2nd edition, revised and enlarged, ND.

Perry, Bliss. *The Heart of Emerson's Journals.* Boston: Houghton Mifflin, 1926.

Porte, Joel. *Emerson in His Journals.* Cambridge, Mass.: The Belknap Press of the Harvard University Press, 1982.

Rawson, Philip, and Laszlo Legeza. *Tao: The Chinese Philosophy of Time and Change.* London: Thames and Hudson, 1979.

Red Pine. *Lao-tzu's Taoteching: Translated by Red Pine with Selected Commentaries of the Past 2000 Years.* San Francisco: Mercury House, 1996.

Richardson, Robert D., Jr. *Emerson: The Mind on Fire.* Berkeley: University of California Press, 1995.

Richter, Gregory C. *The Gate of All Marvelous Things: A Guide to Reading the Tao Te Ching.* San Francisco: Red Mansions Publishing, 1998.

Roberts, Moss. *Dao De Jing: The Book of the Way.* Berkeley: University of California Press, 2001.

Star, Jonathan. *Tao Te Ching: The Definitive Edition by Lao Tzu: Translation and Commentary by Jonathan Star.* New York: Jeremy P. Tarcher/Penguin, 2003.

Waley, Arthur. *Three Ways of Thought in Ancient China.* 1939. London: George Allen & Unwin, 1963.

_____. *The Way and Its Power: A Study of the Tao Te Ching and Its Place in Chinese Thought.* New York: Grove Press, 1958.

_____. *The Analects of Confucius.* New York: Random House, 1938.

Watson, Burton. *Chuang Tzu: Basic Writings.* New York and London: Columbia University Press, 1964.

Watts, Alan, with Chungliang Al Huang. *Tao: The Watercourse Way.* New York: Pantheon Books, 1975.

Welch, Holmes. *Taoism: The Parting of the Way.* Boston: Beacon Press, 1966.

Wu, John C. H. *Tao Te Ching by Lao Tzu.* Boston: Shambhala, 1989.

ACKNOWLEDGMENTS

The magnificent calligraphy in this book is the work and the gift of my old friend Chungliang Al Huang, a Taoist master, author, musician, dancer, and internationally known teacher of Tai Ji and the art of Chinese writing. Of his many books, the first, *Embrace Tiger, Return to Mountain,* after remaining in print for thirty-four years in English, is now available in thirteen languages around the world. I am honored by his contribution to *The Tao of Emerson.*

For personal and editorial support, I am especially grateful to Dr. Richard Geldard, a noted Emerson and Transcendentalist scholar, and his associates David Beardsley, Alec Emerson, and Jim Manley at The Ralph Waldo Emerson Institute. This organization maintains the website rwe.org, which provides access on the Internet to every word Emerson ever wrote, including a digital version of the complete Journals. No one can engage in the serious study of Emerson without using this invaluable resource. I have been the beneficiary of an extraordinary amount of such assistance with this project.

I am continually grateful to Jill Kneerim of Kneerim & Williams for her steady, patient, and always enthusiastic shepherding of my books from idea to publication.

My thanks, too, to those who have given me willing and invaluable help in the development of this book: David Ebershoff, W. S. Merwin, Jon Swan, Larry Volper, Paul de Paolo, Deborah Smith, Ron Ragusa, my colleagues at Smith Farm Center for Healing and the Arts, Jon Umhoefer and The Arts and Humanities Foundation, and my special gratitude to my editor, Judy Sternlight, for her understanding and collegiality in the production of a complex book.

Always at the end of lists like these, but always preeminently first in providing help and wisdom whenever I need them, I thank my wife, Ann Arensberg.

About the Editor

RICHARD GROSSMAN is a psychotherapist, medical educator, essayist, and former book editor and publisher who taught about Taoism and Emerson for many years as associate professor of humanities at New York University and Hunter College. He has also been on the faculty of the Albert Einstein College of Medicine and the Residency Program in Urban Family Medicine at Beth Israel Medical Center.

He was contributing editor to *Health* magazine for ten years, and his articles on health and psychology have appeared in dozens of medical journals and popular magazines. Among his six previous books are *Bold Voices, Choosing and Changing,* and *A Year with Emerson,* which was awarded the Umhoefer Prize in 2006 for achievement in the humanities by the Arts and Humanities Foundation. He is married to the novelist Ann Arensberg and lives in Salisbury, Connecticut.

A NOTE ON THE TYPE

The principal text of this Modern Library edition was
set in Fairfield, the first typeface from the hand of the
distinguished American artist and engraver Rudolph Ruzicka
(1883–1978). In its structure Fairfield displays the sober and
sane qualities of the master craftsman whose talent has long
been dedicated to clarity. It is this trait that accounts for the
trim grace and vigor, the spirited design and sensitive balance,
of this original typeface.